THE WORST OF MINDSPORT

THE WORST OF
MINDSPORT

MUKUL SHARMA

Rupa & Co.
CALCUTTA
ALLAHABAD BOMBAY DELHI

© Mukul Sharma 1992

An Original Rupa Paperback
First published 1992

Published by
Rupa & Co
15 Bankim Chatterjee Street, Calcutta 700 073
135 South Malaka, Allahabad 211 001
P. G. Solanki Path, Lamington Road, Bombay 400 007
7/16 Ansari Road, Daryaganj, New Delhi 110 002

Cover and inside illustrations by Baiju Parthan
Mindsport logo by Anil Aggrawal

Typeset in 10/11 Baskerville by
Megatechnics
19A Ansari Road
New Delhi 110 002

Printed by
Gopsons Papers Pvt Ltd
A-28, Sector IX
Noida 201 301

Rs 50

ISBN 81-7167-096-2

This book is respectfully dedicated to me
for all the help, understanding
and patience I have received from myself
over these long, lunatic years

CONTENTS

INTRODUCTION

Stupid men are a bore.

One can just about suffer a stupid woman, if she is rich and beautiful. But there is nothing to redeem a stupid man, *particularly* if he is rich and beautiful.

That is why when I took over *The Illustrated Weekly of India* as its publisher in the winter of 1982 and (less than a year later) as its editor, my first job (as I saw it) was to make it an intelligent person's magazine.

Among the first things I did was to phone my friend (and neighbour for many years in Calcutta) Mukul Sharma and ask him to start an intelligent games column.

Mukul and I went back many years.

For instance, only one of us finished college. After finishing school at CBS, Mukul went to the Presidency (one of the country's best colleges) but only to woo Aparna Sen, who had just become famous as Satyajit Ray's heroine of *Teen Kanya*. I went there as well in the hope of learning Ouspensky's law of probability (in the undergrad course for statistics) because someone had told me I could improve my odds on the race course if I knew it well enough.

I split when I discovered that (surprise, surprise) the law of probability always gave you a 50 per cent chance of striking failure. Fate then made us neighbours. He and his wife Rina One, as we affectionately called her, lived one floor down from me and my wife Rina Two on the ninth floor of Sonali in Alipore Park Road. Rina Zero, my first wife, had divorced me by then.

We also shared a common publisher for our poems. P Lal.

When M J Akbar, a very dear friend of both of us and Mukul's classmate in CBS, decided to launch *The Telegraph*, Mukul and I teamed up to do the front page pocket cartoon for almost two years. I drew. He wrote the gags. Sometimes it was vice versa. I edited the books page. He wrote The Twilight Zone column.

In between, we planned a poetry magazine that never took off.

He set up a pest control company that lasted the whole of one year.

We often discussed stories and then wrote them independently, to see who could work out a better ending.

He drank himself silly, smoked pot and (generally) had a great time while I was high on living. I poked fun at his moral universe. He ridiculed my obsession to be happy.

We kept sharpening our wits on each other, and on those hapless creatures we bumped into once in a while. So sharp were our attacks that most of them never came our way again. Since I loved being left alone, it did not matter.

Suddenly, one fine morning, right in the midst of planning a voyage by ship from Lisbon to Calicut, following Vasco da Gama's route, I upped and left Calcutta on an invitation from Ashok Jain to join the Times of India Group and run its ailing magazines division.

I hated leaving my beautiful home in Sonali. The books, the paintings, the music. The wonderful Jatin Das across the living room wall.

I hated leaving my old mother, who was living all by herself in a small flat in Park Circus with the memories of my father, and my son Kushan who lived with Rina Zero.

I hated leaving Calcutta, which meant so much to me.

But truly speaking, what I hated most was not having someone like Sharma around to sharpen my wits on.

To punish myself, I left behind the best part of my library in Calcutta. The books on mathematics, philosophy, poetry and Zen. Martin Gardner, Scot Morris, Robert Pirsig, Frank Capra, Douglas Hofstadter, Raymond Smullyan, Lorca, Aragon, Paz, Ginsberg, Faiz, Plath. Without Sharma, who would I discuss poetry with or practise my wit on?

Well, the opportunity came when I introduced Mindsport and it became the blockbuster of a column that it was till I left *The Illustrated Weekly of India* a few months back.

A couple of years later, Sharma quit Calcutta and came over to join me in Bombay, as the editor of *Science Today* (now known as *2001*) of which I was the publisher. He transformed the journal into the most scintillating science magazine in the land. His Mindsport column became a talking point for all those who enjoyed massaging their brains at least once a week, every Friday when *The Illustrated Weekly of*

India hit the stands.

A few months back, I divorced the old lady of Boribunder.

Mukul Sharma did the same last week and is now going over to the *registan* of Dubai, to join another wife this time, the beautiful and multi-talented Binita Mohanty who is a general manager in a multinational garment company there and who (I presume) will be his meal ticket for the next few years as Sharma takes a well-earned sabbatical from full time writing.

The Mindsport column will now appear in *The Sunday Observer* (one of the papers I edit) to stake its claim as one of the most durable (and popular) columns in the history of Indian publishing. A column that never failed to live up to the expectations of its thousands of readers nationwide.

I have travelled all over India over the past decade. Wherever I have been, in every nook and cranny of this vast country, I have met at least one ardent admirer of Mukul Sharma and Mindsport. One man or woman who bought and read *The Illustrated Weekly of India only* for that one column. Rich men. Poor men. Teachers, businessmen, film stars, journalists, smart-arsed politicians, admiring school kids, thieves, whores. There are Mindsport clubs today. There are publishers falling over each other to bring out books on brain games.

But this is the real thing.

Mukul Sharma's Mindsport.

The smartest, funniest, nicest column around today.

I must have been a clever guy to set it going.

Pritish Nandy

PREFACE

Cogito ergo tum : I think, therefore you are.

I'm not responsible for the bunch of lies in the Intro you just read. I'm not responsible for what follows either. A former editor of the *Illustrated Weekly of India* whose first name begins with a P and ends with an H, with five loopholes in between, is the guy you're looking for. You want to complain, complain to him. Chances are he'll pretend to be colour blind, born deaf or brain dead. Or at a meeting.

Like this isn't your friendly neighbourhood quiz time so don't expect original earth-shattering problems in quantum chromodynamics or transactional grammar to which I then supply neat, easy-to-understand solutions guaranteed to leave you gasping with clarity. The scam here is totally different. What problems are here are here courtesy so many years of assiduous swiping from so many sources that if I had to acknowledge even ten per cent of them, they'd end up filling ninety per cent of the rest of the pages. Besides landing me in the slammer, of course.

And talking of answers, I'm not to be blamed for those either because they have all been supplied by readers whose names I have sinfully provided so you know who to sock it to. The cover illustration and other supporting graphics have luckily been taken care of by Baiju Parthan who is the greatest illustrator in the whole world, while two incredibly lovely women called Shehnaaz Rajan and Mildred Braganza take full responsibility for any mistakes in keying in the text. So do Dionezia H Fernandez and Ashok Choudhary for rendering all visuals user-friendly. This leaves some insignificant residual glitches which can conveniently be faulted to Rupa & Company.*

So what in sweet hell is my contribution, right?

---

* Who are you fooling? Ed.

God only knows, except that because I write so well, without me, this book wouldn't be worth the phrase it was turned on.

See what I mean?

MS

MINDSPORT

I
EXHAUSTED FANS

An unusual problem cropped up the other day when for some mystical reason some people who work where I work came to the conclusion that the air in the room where I sit was not conditioned enough. So they wanted to install a machine to do the needful. There was only one hassle. Apparently my room is surrounded by what is called 'workspace' on all four sides. And this machine — in the process of Pavloving the atmosphere — must needs eject hot air. But workspaces have workpeople who dislike any additional warmth other than the natural bonhomie they generate themselves. The atmospheric behaviorists thus decided there was no future in their school of thinking and were about to throw in the towel to the gestaltists when I saw a solution.

"Whose room adjacents mine?" I asked.

"The doctor's," they chorused.

"Does he have an ac?"

"You better believe it," they chortled.

"And it conditions the air in his room?"

They "yup-ped" in unison.

"Any kind of air?"

"Yessir!"

"Then what's wrong in having the hot air exhaust from my ac go into his room?" I asked. "After all, his machine's job is to cool it no matter how hot the going gets. Right guys?"

I thought I had cinched it,

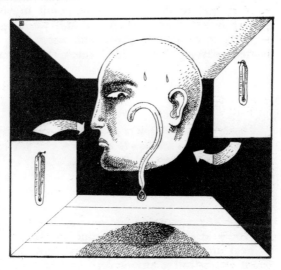

17

but one of them comes back with a "it'll-simply-put-an-extra-load-on-the-machine-and-the-thing-may-conk" kind of rejoinder.

I had him there too. I said, "In that case let the two machines share the load. Let his exhaust be in my room and let mine be in his! That way we can neutralize the 'extra' load."

Naturally, confronted by such awesome genius, some of them swooned, some opted for psychoanalysis and a few, I was told, started believing in life after death.

But, was I right?

FORUM

Dear MS,

Actually I fail to see the problem at all. An airconditioner is supposed to 'condition' the air to whatever temperature setting the thermostat has been set on. And up to reasonable limits, no matter how warm the air is in the room, it should theoretically cool it to that setting. But I have a problem here (*Wait a minute, I'm supposed to be setting the problems here, — MS*) because if your airconditioner's hot exhaust air was being pumped into the doctor's room then his airconditioner's exhaust would be hotter than normal because of the extra work it had to do. This would result in your exhaust also getting hotter than normal and this would go on repeatedly — each room getting more and more hot — till you both started roasting. No, I don't think there is any solution.

Yours thoughtfully,
Anjali Mitra, IIM, Calcutta

Thanks a lot AM, you're great. You've got to be the only person I know who has no solution to a problem that you can't see. Life must be one big ball for you at IIM.

Dear MS,

Since any airconditioner works by taking away heat from the room, if there is another one sneaking in equal quantities of heat into the room at the same time, the poor guy in the room won't find it any cooler. And back to back reminds me of the two guys who decided to avoid getting a suntan by hiding in each other's shadow!

Yours solvingly,
Sachi, Bombay

II
COPY, T OR ME?

Look, there's a friend I have called Partha Basu, who had nothing to do with this except that he has a deep base voice for booming out incorrect answers; two daughters who I frequently charm the pants off; one gorgeous wife who doesn't look like a Sindhi even though she isn't one and he once lent me a book that contained this problem. You want to complain, complain to his nuclear unit. It goes like this:

Solve this in your mind without using a diagram or a model. Imagine that you put two pieces of typing paper on your desk with a piece of carbon paper between them, as if you wanted to write something in duplicate. Now, imagine that you fold this assembly in half with the crease running left to right, bringing the lower-half back under the top. If you write the letter T on the top-half of the top sheet, how many copies will you make, where will they appear (front, back, top, bottom, first sheet, second sheet), and how will they be oriented?

Okay, you can cheat.

FORUM

Dear MS,

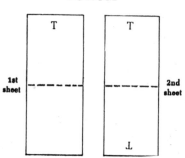

In the position you have mentioned, if you put a T on the top half of the top sheet, you will get three copies in all (1 + 2). One on the top-half front of the top sheet; two on the second sheet (carbon copies) — front side only — one on top-half (and an exact copy of the first), and then another on bottom-half but vertically inscribed.

Yours sincerely,
J V Ramanamurty, Madras

III

LIVE ROULETTE DIE

Like I've had it up to here (I'm pointing to my chin) with everybody going how easy my problems are and how it takes them only a couple of years to solve them, etc. So, therefore, now ladies and gentlemen, I present a little gift of the grab to you.

A man plays a game of Russian Roulette (that's when you put in one bullet in the chamber of a revolver, spin the cylinder, and lock it, so that there's no way of knowing if  the bullet is in the breech or not when you aim it at your nut and squeeze the trigger; five to one you'll live) in the following way: he puts two bullets in a six chamber cylinder and pulls the trigger twice. The cylinder is spun before the first shot, but it may or may not be spun after putting in the first bullet and after taking the first shot.

Which of the following situations produces the lowest probability of survival?

  (a) Spinning the cylinder after loading the first bullet, and spinning again after the first shot.

  (b) Spinning the cylinder after loading the first bullet only.

  (c) Spinning the cylinder after firing the first shot only.

  (d) Not spinning the cylinder either after loading the first bullet or after the first shot.

  (e) The probability is the same for all cases.

No foxy answers like "Oh it's (a)" or "(c) of course". I want good, hard, solid reasoning behind your solution. Not that I expect one before five years. That's also about when I'll tell you where I got that one from.

FORUM

Dear MS,

I am not certain whether this will reach you before five years, 'cause you know what our postal system is like. But believe me you, I saw the problem this morning and have been looking at it a few minutes only. An ' I won't say how many seconds it took me to figure this out because honestly, Sharmaji, I don't want to hurt your ego (*It's okay, it's gone into terminal flatulence — MS*).

Well, the lowest probability of survival arises from situation (b) and here is why:

Situation (a): The probability of our hero surviving the 1st shot is 4/6 or 2/3. And since he spins the cylinder after firing the 1st shot the chance of his surviving the second shot is again 2/3. Hence the probability of surviving situation (a) is 2/3 × 2/3 = 4/9.

Situation (b): The probability of his surviving the 1st shot is 2/3 and that of the 2nd shot is 3/5 (since three of the remaining five chambers are unloaded). Hence the probability of surviving situation (b) is 2/3 × 3/5 = 2/5.

Situation (c): The probability of surviving the 1st shot is 2/3 and since he spins the cylinder after this, the probability of surviving the next shot is again 2/3, and hence of surviving situation (c) is 4/9.

Situation (d): The probability of surviving the 1st shot is 2/3.

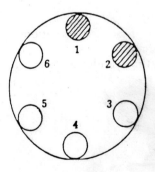

Now since the bullets are loaded in consecutive chambers, the man will die from the second shot only if he had fired chamber 6 the first time. Thus the probability of surviving the second shot is 3/4 and of surviving situation (d) is 2/3 × 3/4 = 1/2.

Clearly situation (b) has the lowest probability of survival.

Yours affectionately,
Udai Bajaj, Lucknow

IV

HAVE A BALL

So here's this guy called Bhaskar Bose who's another weird friend of mine (yes I have normal friends too but they're in jail most of the time) and he comes over to my house three days back and the first thing I do is go for his throat saying, "Give me a puzzle! Give me a good puzzle! Give me at least a semi-original good puzzle! There's a billion people outside this page panting for blood."

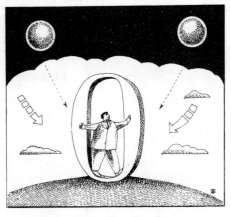

After he's disentangled me from his neck he reaches in his pocket and ups a Cartier femto-tip and asks for paper. I hand him a ream. His strokes go like this:

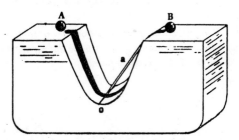

I've given the original here and you can easily make out he's of the post abstract-expressionist school. Anyway, the whole thing is a block of wood with a catenary section cut out from the top. A catenary incidentally is the curve described by any freely hanging cable from two ends. You could hold a thin chain in your own two index fingers and thumbs and get the same shape from the suspension which is the result solely of gravity.

25

"O" is the lowest point: "A" is a straight plank of wood lying on one side. The curved section on the left has a groove cut in it down the middle. So has the plank. The two grooves are identical in shape and things. "a" and "b" are two small balls identical in shape, size, weight, etc. They are released simultaneously: "a" rolls down the curve, "b" down the plank. Which ball reaches O first?

FORUM

Dear MS,

Friction (hope you know it) being the same for both your balls (*Hey what's happening?* — *MS*) they should take the same time for rolling down to point O. Reason: It is (the) height through which they fall that matters, not the track or trail. Time taken for each ball (by conservation of mechanical energy), i.e., equate initial potential energy + initial kinetic energy to final potential energy + kinetic energy, blah, blah, blah.

Yours sportingly,
Jeetendra Jain, Hyderabad

Quite right. But only one person cottoned on to the catch in the question (though that's got nothing to do with the answer) — that none of the balls would reach the bottom point.

Dear MS,

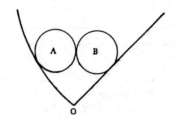

26

As per the theory of motion of projectiles, two objects having equal mass and equal potential energy, dropped from a certain height will reach the surface of the earth at the same time acting only on gravitational force, whatever the path they may follow. Thus the two identical balls dropped at the same time from the top of the wooden block (one down the grooved curved surface and the other along the grooved straight sloping surface) will reach the bottom of the slopes at the same time. As the balls (have a) spherical surface, they would meet each other just above point O which is the bottommost point, and not literally on point O as in the diagram on p. 26.

V Balasubramanian, Baroda

Quite right my ass! Along with 43 other worthies who embraced the cause of the ball on the catenary curve cascading down at the same time as the one on the straight path, I too in my blissful vapidity assumed the same till this stinker snowballed into my head.

Dear MS,

Balls to you! I should say that the time taken for the balls A and B to reach the bottom need not be the same. In the diagram given below, ball A would definitely overtake ball B

though both are at the same height above the ground.

It can be proved that the velocity of the two balls just before they reach the bottom is equal. However, the time taken to reach the bottom depends very much on the nature of the paths taken by them.

Yours criticisingly,
V Raman, Madras

In this connection, B C Roy of Behrampur, West Bengal, points out that though V Balasubramanian is correct in saying that objects having equal mass and equal potential energy dropped from a certain height will reach the surface of the earth at the same time, the problem here is that the balls are not falling freely. They are not only acted on by gravity, but also by forces of constraints due to the grooved inclined plane in one case and a grooved curved surface in another.

However, the original frazzle still remains: which ball reaches point O first? Remember that a working model on similar lines is on display at the Sir Visheshvarayya Technological Museum at Bangalore, and that there the ball rolling down the curve reaches first, even though S Lakshmipathi of Rajahmundry still insists that "Though it is true that the time taken will be the same ... everybody is wrong because for all curves other than the catenary the time will be different." Maybe we should wait for his solution.

(Although SL's solution has not come in till date and I myself have no idea what the answer is, I recently saw a definition of a catenary curve, a part of which I thought might be important and should perhaps have been mentioned when the problem was first set: "A curve formed by a uniform chain hanging freely from two points not in the same vertical line.")

28

V

THE EGGSACTNESS OF LOGIC

What you will need: 2 boxes; 1 egg; several smart alecs; some finesse.

What to do: Tell the alec who looks the smartest to put the egg in one of the boxes while your back's turned, such that when you open the boxes in sequence (say from left to right) the placement of the egg should surprise you. Then announce that (s)he can never surprise you as to where that egg is. When the hysterical sniggers die down explain calmly why not, and leave a pall of silence behind you as you exit humming a snatch of some old song.

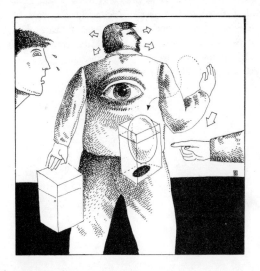

How it is done: Consider the two boxes. According to the conditions laid down you have to open box A first, correct? Obviously, the person couldn't have been that much of a schmuck to have placed the egg there, right? Meaning if it was in A there wouldn't be any surprise element left, would there? Therefore (s)he has to put it in box B which isn't a surprise either, since by now you're expecting it to be there, considering it can't be in box A. That's all. Only remember never ever to actually open any of those boxes in real life because you'll be surprised how surprised you can be. So how come this impeccable logic differs from reality?

FORUM

I have no idea why this is so and no one ever got back to me either. Meanwhile here's an interesting extrapolation. Teacher says to his class on Saturday that there's going to be a surprise test sometime next week, meaning either on Mon, Tue, Wed, Thu, Fri or Sat but while everyone is buried in whatever books they slam into you in school over the weekend, Our Man Flint's watching funnies on TV. When mom wants to know why in sweet heaven he isn't on the ball he says because there can't be no surprise test. Oh yeah, says his mother, and how in hell so? So he replies that, see, it can't be on the last day of the week because if the test hasn't been held Mon thru Fri then it has to be on Sat. But then it's not a surprise any more. Meaning Sat can be safely ruled out. Now the last day of the week becomes Friday. But by the same reasoning if the test has not been held Mon thru Thu then it has to be on Fri. Again no surprise.

Same reasoning all the way up to Mon.

THE THIRD WORD WAR

The ditty goes: Thirty days has September/April, June and November/All the rest have thirty one/Except February alone/And that has twenty eight days clear/And twenty nine in each leap year. The easy question is — quickly now — how many months have thirty days? Answer: all months have thirty days except February. The tough question is — take your time — what special quality does the word TWEN-TYNINE have when it is written in all caps? Incidentally it is the *only* number to have it.

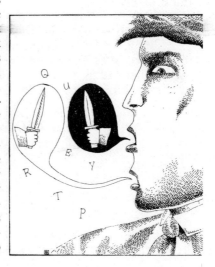

Here/are/some/fast/ones/now. There's another word in common use which usually describes a person or thing as not to be found in any place whatsoever, and yet, with no alteration other than a mere space between syllables it voltefaces and correctly describes that person or thing as being actually present at the very moment. The second longest word that can be constructed using only the top QWERTYUIOP line of a typewriter is — get this — TYPEWRITER! The longest is an eleven letter word. You figure that. I'll only tell you that FLASKS is the longest possible on the second row. Doubled letters in words like bOOk, pEEk, suMMer, hiTTing are common. Less so are witHHold, skIIng, BooKKeeper and vacUUm. Got any incorporating VV and WW? Okay naVVy is one of them.

IVANHOE, BY SIR WALTER SCOTT can be anagrammed to produce "a novel by a Scottish writer" but who cares?

HOARSE, LAMB, CZAR, HANDSOME, TWITCHED, NEUFCHATEL, GNOME, MYRRH, HEIFER, MARIJUANA, KNIGHT, TALK, MNEMONIC, AUTUMN, LEOPARD,

PSYCHOLOGIST, CINQ-CENTS, ATELIER, VISCOUNT, LISTEN, PLAQUE, WRITING, CHATEAUX, PRAY and RENDEZVOUS have something in common in alphabetical order. What is it and why is V not represented? Can you think of one for V?

794 letters are used to make up the words for the numbers one through ninety-nine. But not only is L used only twice; J, K, M, P, Q & Z are not used at all. And if you thought those were sidey letters then know that D, C, B & A are not used either. In fact how far do you think you might have to count before encountering an A?

FORUM

This one seems to have fascinated everyone into not only giving correct answers but correcting crept-in errors and suggesting novelties. The special quality TWENTYNINE has, when written in all caps, is that is has exactly twenty-nine straight strokes comprising it. NOWHERE with a gap between syllables such as in NOW HERE becomes its exact opposite. K Balagopalan Nair of Trivandrum informs us that the eleven letter word using only the top line of the typewriter is RUPTUREWORT, a kind of plant, if that qualifies, though I don't see why not. Another word incorporating WW is GLOWWORM according to Ashoke Roy, although this is sometimes hyphenated. And Kalpana Rao of Bangalore says that there is a word where though V is not really silent, it is at least pronounced differently as in VELD. G M Bhatt of Osmanabad adds that regarding words like BEDECKED, ICEBOX, CHOICE, KIDDED, etc: "A straight line passing through their middles cuts the word into two mirror images. If the upper half is kept on a mirror, the complete word reappears again." And I'm sorry but you have to count up to a thousand to run across the first "A". One hundred and one will not do because the user-correct form is without the conjunction like in cheques. At least I think so.

VII

THE TIMES THEY ARE A-CHAINING

When you were slightly younger than what you're older than that now — say about ten or so or more years ago — wasn't it true that every time you hit that highway you were bound to see those massive aviation fuel tankers lumbering and looming up the windscreen for your car to honk and pass? And wasn't it also true that just when you did pass you saw this bit of chain hanging attached to the back of the tanker's body dangling just down to the asphalt? When I asked my daddy what it was for he said it was to earth the vehicle. Like if there was a spark or something then that would get grounded and we wouldn't have a roasted truck to pass. When I pointed out to him that the chain hitting bits of metal fragments on the surface of the road was itself generating sparks from time to time and could lead to a broiler on wheels he told me to shaddap and keep reading my Bugs Bunny comics or he'd whup the ass off/a me.

But whatever; how/come we don't see these chains any more?

After all, the contact between the tyres and the road still leaves the tyres negatively charged, and as they rotate and become uniformly charged, the negative electrons in the metal

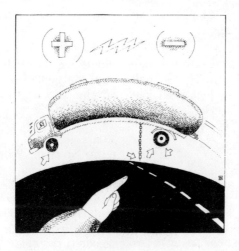

body and frame are repelled by the tyres, leaving the body area near them positively charged. Sparking between a particular part of the vehicle and some nearby grounded or oppositely charged body is also still possible. Chains used to be dragged from the truck's body to the ground because they would then continuously discharge the truck. Why has this practice been stopped?

FORUM

Dear MS,

I hate you and therefore have this answer which is a question. What do you think happens to the millions of tyres which are worn out every year from all kinds of vehicles? Where do those millions of tons of rubber go to? Surely not the atmosphere or we would have had vulcanized lungs by now. They are all deposited on the road's surface itself and that makes the road's surface a non-conductor. And that is why chains are no longer needed.

Yours sincerely,
Ras Behari Das, Bhubaneshwar

I agree; good question there RBD. Where for the love of Mike does all that rubber go to?

Dear MS,

Contact between the tyres and the ground did not leave the tyres positively or negatively charged. Because rubber does not conduct electricity. So the use of the chain was needless.

Yours etc,
Arun Srivatsh, Bangalore

Actually, according to the Transactions of the American Institute of Electrical Engineers *in an article generously subtitled "Generation of Electric Charges by Moving Rubber-Tyred Vehicles" (62; 207), S S Mackeown and V Wouk affirm that "Contact between the tyres and road leaves the tyres negatively charged.... The sparking*

34

would be merely a nuisance except in the case of petrol trucks where petrol fumes may be ignited. Years ago chains were dragged from a truck's body and on the ground in the belief that the chains would continuously discharge the truck. The chain would drain some of the electrons from the truck's body, but that would not leave the truck neutral and thus safe because it would then be positively charged and hence still susceptible to sparking."

VIII
THE COMPLEAT PARADOX

Godelian Incompleteness Theoremist: (pointing at the stars) Hey schmuck, what do you think is the probability of life existing in some form or the other on that dark companion of Barnard's star?

You: (reeking of probability theory) Oh, I don't know. I guess the possibility of life or no life is equally likely. I'd say half.

GIT: Okay, let's look at it another way. How would you rate the probability of no elephants there?

You: Gee, I really don't know. Half again, I reckon.

GIT: And the probability of giant sloths?

You: Half too?

GIT: What about aardvarks?

You: (panicking) Hey, I've got to go home now. It's getting late and ...

GIT: Go on, take an educated guess.

You: All right damn it, half once more!

(This goes on for a while with GIT naming, say, 17 more forms of life, while you're "halfing" away like your mouth was full of 0.5s)

GIT: (succinctly summing up) Right then; so should we conclude that the probability of all these things occurring at once — no elephants and no giant sloths and no aardvarks and none of the other 17 forms of life I mentioned — is the product of the individual probabilities, or $(\frac{1}{2})$ $(\frac{1}{2})$ $(\frac{1}{2})$ ... to 20 terms? In other words, the probability that none of these 20 forms of life exists is $(\frac{1}{2})^{20}$ or $1/1048576$. Am I right or am I right?

You: (perspiring freely) Er, yessir, you sure are.

GIT: I thought so. But if the probability that none of these forms of life exists is 1/1048576, what may I ask, is the probability that *at least one* of them exists?

You: (cowering in abject logistics) This is going to land me in a load of nightsoil your honour, but the probability is the difference between your result and 1. I mean 1048575/1048576.

GIT: You said it, goof. And now we're led to two results concerning the probability of life on that there dark companion of Barnard's star. One's 0.5, and the other's about 0.999999, which is almost a sure thing. You think your graduate course needs revision, nerd?

Okay, you probability theorists, what do you think?

FORUM

Dear MS,

We are sending the remaining part of the dialogue between the Godelian Incompleteness Theoremist and Me which you failed to publish in your 'Incomplete Paradox'.

Me: (looking for a club to dent GIT's skull) Hey GIT, you nitwit, compare the existence of life to the occurrence of a head in a coin toss. Taking just one coin the probability of the head is 0.5. Here we're conducting a simple experiment and the sample space consists of only two sample points. Similarly the existence of at least one animal is reduced to the occurrence of at least one head in 20 events with the new sample space consisting of 20 (20) point(s). In the above cases, the sample spaces are different and hence there is no room for comparison, nerd.

GIT: (burying himself in the sand) Ummm ... ?

Me: Don't bury facts, bury yourself.

In all probability,

Yours insincerely,
T V Ganesh & Ajay
Sharma, Delhi

IX
THE FALLING SHADOW

Week before last I was mad at Indian Airlines for serving me *idlis* for the tenth consecutive flight. Hell, I have nothing against southie fast food — in fact, I've been caught secretly lacing *masala dosas* with crack on several occasions — but this was the limit. First thing I did when I got off that craft was ring up my friend Patu (ya, it's a weird name; short for Patanjali) who's apparently in charge of all the aerial entrées and told him to move his ass over and treat me to dinner at a 5* or I'd pour *rasam* down his neck. He immediately agreed and then proceeded to scour the city's hotel registers to find which common friend was staying in one of them till he located one — the cheapo.

Then he comes over to my place in the evening with his beautiful wife श (ya, that's the name; short for Sharanita, but I don't know how to spell it, though it's pronounced like) and the four of us shuffled over to Bingo's (God knows where they pick up their names from; must be the Polish yellow pages — anyway it's short for Binganjali, the ninth century humorist who died of tonsillitis) hotel and generally had quite a toot till Patu, who thinks he's smarter than I picks up a pencil and draws these three figures.

They are shadows, he says, in the shape of a square, a circle and a triangle, as if I thought they were in the shape of hexagons, rhombuses and parallelograms, and wants to know what single three-dimensional solid, oriented differentwise, can cast them?

Please let's have the solutions accompanied by your carefully sketched inartistic diagrams or, as usual, I'll be left miasmaing in a bunch of syntactical geometry.

And while we're on this (on what? I thought we were talking about Dravidian dishes and shadows) did you know that a square hole can be drilled? In fact, there is actually a patent out for this drill and it can be purchased. Any ideas what the bit looks like?

FORUM

Dear MS,

Take a tube of Binaca toothpaste, or for that matter Signal (if a railman) or Flash (if a photographer) and so on. Shaving tubes will do equally well. Use it for some days and squeeze out half of the tube. (If rich, open out the hindquarters of the tube.) Then form a triangle out of it. With the cap on (not the Derby type) (*Please remember all this corn is coming from him, not me — MS*) and seen front-on it is a circle; seen sideways it is a square; and seen from behind, a triangle.

There you have it. All that has to be done to make a solid out of it is cast it in gold and see if you can get it past the customs claiming it to be a scientific achievement. I get a percentage if you're successful.

Yours etc,
Sujay Gopal Rao, Madras

Samir Mathur of Haryana had a curious observation to make in this connection. He says that if a solid object can be interpreted to mean a fabricated object which uses space in its own way then to have a look at the following object

39

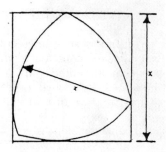

which *Joshua Sunil Sikhamani of Cochin has sketched.*

All this, of course while R K Kaul of Faridabad has a bit (groan) of good news about the square drill. A square hole, he says, can be produced by a drill with a special profile and a stem designed to float in a holder and controlled by a guide plate.

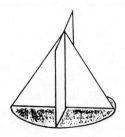

The cutting portion of this drill controlled by the guide plate moves in a series of apparent jerky motions, allowing the corners of the drill to be forced into the corners of the guide plate aperture.

X
HIGH CUBE

The policy of this column is so evanescent and puerile that yours truly feels no pang of conscience whatsoever in totally *maaroing* a problem that appeared only a few months back in *Omni* magazine. (Though a word of praise here for the editor for running it in the face of a probable lawsuit. Thanks Ed).

But can I help it if the problem is so good and so tough? And this time the test they ran was discriminating at the 99.9999th percentile which is roughly an IQ of 164 and above. Apparently, people who can pass this test can belong to a group called the Mega Society which is recognized by the Guinness folk as "the world's most exclusive IQ society". Thus with just one word of caution belonging to a well-known psychologist who said, quite profoundly, "IQ tests only measure how well a person does in IQ tests," let's get on with the plagiarisation.

Suppose that each side of a cube is painted a single uniform colour — red, blue, or yellow — such that any two sides painted red are chromatically indistinguishable, as are any two painted blue or any two painted yellow. When all six

sides are visualized simultaneously, they constitute a colour pattern for the cube. Two colour patterns are mutually indistinguishable whenever one can be made to coincide with the other by suitable rigid rotations. For example, there is only one distinguishable colour pattern consisting of one blue side and five yellow sides. How many distinguishable colour patterns can a cube have, counting all six sides in each pattern and assuming that each side must be painted red, blue, or yellow?

That make any sense to you? It sure as hell don't to me.

FORUM

Five replies in all. Wow, what a stunning figure! And only two correct (one of them on the second attempt) I think. I say I think because I figured — like Harshad Abhyankar — it was 56, till Harshad's second attempt pointed out to me what pattern I had missed and would have never guessed: a mirror image possibility. Vivek Jain was the only one who got it right the first time: 57. Let Baroda's Frankie explain.

Dear MS,

Combination	Patterns	
6	3	(3 × 1)
1-5	6	(6 × 1)
2-4	12	(6 × 2)
3-3	6	(3 × 2)
1-2-3	18	(6 × 3)
1-1-4	6	(3 × 2)
2-2-2	5	*(here's where you goofed it — MS)*
Total	56	

Judging by the type of tests you run I think you have an IQ of around 125. Above average certainly, but nothing very great.

Yours etc,
Frankie of Baroda

Judging by your solution Frankie, join the club. Listen to this instead first, though.

Dear MS,

This orientation of the 2-2-2 combination consists of three hinges, one of each colour, and its mirror image. These two mirror images cannot be transformed into one another by rigid rotations.

Yours sincerely,
Harshad Abhyankar

XI

SETTING A PRESIDENT

Consider the 16th and 35th presidents of the United States — Abraham Lincoln and John F Kennedy.

1. Both were elected to Congress exactly a hundred years apart (1846::1946).
2. Both were elected to the presidency exactly a hundred year apart (1860::1960).
3. Both were human rights campaigners.
4. Both were assassinated by southerners.
5. Both were shot in the head from behind on a Friday.
6. Both had their wives sitting beside them on the right.
7. Both were succeeded by southerners named Johnson — Andrew and Lyndon (13 letters in each name) — who were born exactly a hundred years apart.
8. Both their respective assassins — John Wilkes Booth and Lee Harvey Oswald (15 letters in each name) — were born exactly a hundred years apart.
9. Both assassins were shot before they could stand trial.
10. Booth shot Lincoln in a theatre and ran to a warehouse; Oswald shot Kennedy from a warehouse and ran to a theatre.
11. Both presidents and their assassins lived for a while after being mortally wounded.

12. Lincoln was shot in Ford's theatre; Kennedy was shot in a Ford Motors car — a Lincoln.

13. Lincoln had a secretary named Kennedy who advised him against going to the theatre; Kennedy had a secretary named Lincoln who advised him not to go to Dallas.

14. Both Lincoln and Kennedy had a premonition of death which they conveyed to their wives.

15. Both assassinations generated mammoth controversies. It is still not definitely established if Oswald and Booth were operating singly or were part of a greater conspiracy.

So I thought while we're on the subject of prime ministers here are the names of 41 US presidents to date: Washington, Adams, Jefferson, Madison, Monroe, Adams, Jackson, Buren, Harrison, Tyler, Polk, Taylor, Fillmore, Pierce, Buchanan, Lincoln, Johnson, Grant, Hayes, Garfield, Arthur, Cleveland, Harrison, Cleveland, McKinley, Roosevelt, Taft, Wilson, Harding, Coolidge, Hoover, Roosevelt, Truman, Eisenhower, Kennedy, Johnson, Nixon, Ford, Carter, Reagan and Bush.

The psychic mafia see in this yet another mysterious bond between presidents. Somehow, each and every president shares something with one president who remains constant. What is this link? And who is the reference point president?

Hah! An original!

FORUM

Dear MS,

Okay so you got an original. So what? I got one too. An original answer to what's common to all presidents of the US with a reference point prexy. It's that every president after Washington (the first chief exec) has had at least one letter in his last name in common with Washington's.

Hah to you too!

Mandakini Shroff, Jammu

(*Since that appeared Bush has succeeded Reagan. But the magic still works. Now if that Duke guy ...*)

45

XII
FREEZE A JOLLY GOOD FELLOW

I'm in a fix. Sometime back I had been unusually snide with my science adviser friend when he had suggested I run the problem of why a container of hot water freezes faster than a container of cold water. I'd told him that was only an old wives' tale and then had run a modified version saying that water which has been heated or boiled before cooling freezes faster than water which has not. The reason I was so sure was because I had recently read in the *Dictionary of Misinformation* that "One of the most enduring folk myths is that a bucket of hot water will freeze faster than a bucket of cold water. It won't. True, water that has been heated or boiled before cooling may freeze faster, because heating or boiling drives out some air bubbles that otherwise inhibit freezing because they cut down on thermal conductivity." (p. 125)

But now apparently new light has dawned on the old problem and my friend's been rubbing fresh salt into my healed wounds. Any takers before I go public?

FORUM

Dear MS,

When cold water is poured into a can before freezing, it contains dissolved air, dissolved bicarbonates, and small entrapped air bubbles sticking to the surface. The air bubbles and dissolved air which is released on freezing act as a barrier to free heat-transfer. The dissolved salts also lower the freezing point. When water is boiled and cooled in the can before freezing, the above problems are not there. Hence freezing is faster. There you are!

Yours faithfully,
Sushmita Narayan, Jabalpur

Yes, but where am I Sushmita? An old foe, who always knows more about more things than I, has surfaced with this letter.

Dear MS,

Up to a certain temperature, hot water does freeze faster than cold water, provided cold water is unboiled and hot water is boiled and cooled to the higher temperature. So you are wrong.

Yours,
S Lakshmipathi, Rajahmundry

Ironically, around this same time, the earlier mentioned man of science, literally seething in indignation at having been stymied by a mere illiterate like me, zapped another book back at my face. A book he claimed was more authoritative than mine. It was The Flying Circus of Physics *by Jearl Walker. Walker, if you throw your mind back you'll remember, was the one who paraded the Leidenfrost effect once upon a time to refute paranormal claims to firewalking fames. Anyway, to cut a long story short, in this book Walker says that it is not an old wives' tale. That even Francis Bacon noticed this and that you can try it right at home in your refrigerator. The reason he gives is that the increased evaporation from the warmer water leads to a*

47

reduction in mass so that the cooling of the hot water overtakes the cooling of the initially cooler water and reaches freezing point first.

Will the real authorities please leave their ten dimensional superstring theories behind and look inside their fridges for our answer?

XIII

MAGNETIC MOMENTS

Okay, here's a little game of inspired ingenuity you can play with yourself when, even though you're feeling like a son of man, the whole world's pushing you out of the shadow of the red rock.

Close your eyes (not now for Christ's sake — after you've finished reading) and conjure up in your mind the image of your favourite room. Now slowly begin to make things vanish from there. All the furniture and all fixtures like conditioners of air, cleaners of vacuums, cookers of ranges, colours of television, carpets, couches, curtains, cushions, closets, cabinets, clothes, cutlery, crockery, kitchenware, commodes, cosmetics, correspondence, cameras, computers, crooks, cutthroats, crabs and whatever the hell else you have in your favourite room till you're left with just four walls, a ceiling, a door and a floor and no windows either please.

Got that so far? Good, now turn that room into a wooden one. No metal nowhere at all. If you have concealed wiring, make that disappear too. Next take off all your clothes and imagine yourself inside the room standing in your birthday suit and holding two identical pieces of metal of the same shape, size, colour, smell, taste, etc. If you think that's going to make you begin to feel like a fool here's another think coming: one of those pieces of metal is a magnet and one of them isn't. Unless you can tell which is which they're neither going to give you your clothes back nor your favourite room.

Besides, outside the same bad world's waiting to show you fear in a handful of dust.

Dear MS,

Take one piece, say A, and place one end of it at the mid-point of the other piece B. If some force of attraction is felt between the two pieces, then A is the magnet, otherwise B is the magnet. The reason is that in a magnet the poles lie at the ends, hence maximum attraction there. In the middle there is no magnetic force. Any eighth-grader science student could have told you that.

Sincerely yours,
A A Talwar, Chandigarh

Ah, but most Mindsport readers aren't eighth-grade pushovers A A. They sit there grimacing like Monty Python and then go in for the kill. Watch carefully as seven other solutions ranging from the textbookesque to the transcendental unfurl in front of your aghast eyes.

Dear MS,

Let's call the piece being held in the subject's right hand A, and the other B. Grasping A firmly, the subject proceeds to rub one of its ends along the length of B, in one direction always. After a while this process is discontinued and B and A are brought end to end. B is then reversed and brought end to end again with A. If both trials produce attraction, then A is an ordinary piece of metal and B, the magnet. If however, one trial produces attraction and the other repulsion between the pieces, a small problem arises. A is the original magnet no doubt, but B, originally your everyday piece of scrap metal, is now magnetized too. This can be cured by dropping it several times on the floor.

Just shriek the next time you need help. Oh, and by the way, I find your page has become an interesting little atrocity.

See you later, alligator,

N Deepak, Rourkela

Dear MS,

Suspend the metal pieces with length(s) of body hair (that from the head — if not bald — is best, or you may have to join several lengths). One of the metal pieces will consistently lie parallel to a certain axis. That will be the bar magnet pointing north-south.

Yours etc,
Ashok Roy, Bombay

Dear MS,

I was stuck with the magnet problem till it struck me that if I struck one bar with the other and broke it into two, I'd have the answer. For, if it was the magnetic bar I broke, I'd have two small magnets which would attract or repel each other depending on the polarity on the ends brought together; whereas if it was the metallic bar I'd broken, the two pieces would neither attract nor repel.

Sincerely yours,
Nupur Prakash, Allahabad

Dear MS,

There is an alternative solution to the problem, based on the principle that the force of attraction exerted by the magnet in the side-on position is greater than that exerted by it in the edge-on position.

Keep one piece A stationary with the index finger and move the other piece B perpendicular to it as shown.

At a certain distance (x) B will move towards A due to the force of attraction. Next, keep A and B along the same

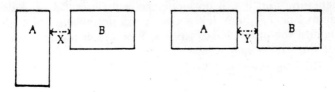

line, again holding A stationary. At a certain distance (y) B will again move towards A. If x = y then B is the magnet. If x is less than y then A is the magnet

Unwillingly yours,
N S Chithambaram, Bombay

Dear MS,

Since you did not put any time limit on how long a guy has before he can tell which is which, I could advise you to try magneto-therapy with each of them in turn. The one which works wonders is your magnet!

It's been a pleasure talking to you and wasting your time.

Yours,
Zahid Hasan, Mirzapur

Dear MS,

It is known now that bees and pigeons have a substance called "magnetite" in their heads which helps them home in on targets like flowers and roosts. It is also postulated that human beings may possess the same thing. So all one has to do is keep two bars at two corners of the room and crawl along the floor with eyes closed towards their mid-point. The bar your head makes contact with is the magnet.

Three cheers for science!

Bryan Callaghan, Ranchi

Dear MS,

If you keep throwing a magnet hard against the floor repeatedly, its domains will ultimately randomize in their orientation and it will no longer be a magnet. So keep doing that to one of them for a couple of hours and then check it against the other. If attraction still occurs, it wasn't a magnet. If it does not, then it was. Simple.

Expecting harder ones.

Renee Baruah, Jorhat

XIV

DUE WEST, YOUNG MAN

I have a suggestion to make. This is not going to sound nice though. But the time has come for tough decisions which feeble men like me have to make. Here goes: will all people who have IQs between 135 and 165 please stop reading this column from today and ignore it fully and finally in future forever? Because otherwise what's happening is that whenever I give some simple problem like why the Roman numeral IV is written as IIII only in clocks and watches I get back monographs on "Testable Incompatibility between Einstein's Locality Condition and Quantum Mechanics with CP Violation." Know what I mean? So I've decided to limit Mindsport to the normal and genius ranges only. Not only are they funner to get along with but they also appreciate the fact that, like them, I'm only a brilliantly mediocre convoluter.

Anyway, with that sizeable portion of readership behind us, let's see if we can rehash something with knobs on.

A man walks 10 miles due south, then 10 miles due west. There he shoots a bear. He then walks 10 miles north. This brings him back to his point of origin. What's the colour of the bear?

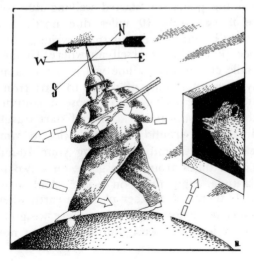

You can stop shouting it's white of course because it's a polar bear because the north pole is the only point from where you can go 10 miles south, then 10 miles west, then 10 miles north and return to your point of origin. However, the reason I run this oldie but goldie is because of some fascinating ramifications (is that the right word?) it has generated. The chief among them is that the north pole (or the south pole with directions reversed) is not the only point on earth where you can do that due south, west, north routine and find yourself standing outside your freezing front door again. There are many more places on earth where this can be done. In fact there are an infinite number of places.

Consider: the circumference of the earth is 25,000 miles. This simply means that the latitude at the equator is 25,000 miles long. All lines of latitude below the equator are shorter in length, and progressively so, till, at the south pole it is a point — i.e. O. But, somewhere between that point at the pole and the equator, there has to be one line of latitude which is exactly 10 miles long. Now, position yourself anywhere 10 miles to the north of that line. Due north, that is. If you start walking due south from there, you'll land up on the line. Start walking due west. You'll go the whole way around and arrive at the point you started walking due west from. From there if you walk 10 miles due north again, why honeychile, that's your homestead there waiting for you.

Also, since positioning yourself anywhere 10 miles north of that 10-mile circumference line will give the same results, you actually have an infinity of points to start from.

A variation of the above is to choose a latitude of five miles length. When you arrive at O and start travelling due west, you'd be going around the earth twice to complete 10 miles to rearrive at O and start doing your 10-mile north trek again. Four times around the globe on a two-and-a-half mile long latitude. Eight times on a 1.25. And so on.

Question: Is there yet another place on earth where, using a different way of reasoning, you can (here we go again) go due south 10 miles ditto west ditto miles, ditto north ditto ditto?

FORUM

Dear MS,

I think this can be done theoretically at least. If you are on a ship (large enough to accommodate the problem) and the ship keeps moving due east at the same speed as your walk when you walk due west after having walked due south, you will come back to your starting point relative to the earth when you walk due north after that.

Yours sincerely,
R Soundararajan, Karur,
Tamil Nadu

Well, that's not really correct, because since the ship is continuously moving, both the north-south and south-north journeys will be greatly skewed. One possible solution would be if the ship only moved during the person's east-west journey. But that's a highly artificial kind of solution. Anyway, good try.

XV
JUST NUT CRICKET

This really has no connection with what we do in this page or the problem I'm about to gas about but I thought I simply had to share it with you to point out that I'm not the only one around breakdancing the English language. Framers of judicial statutes do the same. Have a look at the semantic screwup a judge of the Court of Sessions of Scotland once came across. The Act still exists.

"In the Nuts (unground), (other than ground nuts) Order, the expression 'nuts' shall have reference to such nuts, other than ground nuts, as would but for this amending Order not qualify as nuts (unground) (other than ground nuts) by reason of their being nuts (unground)."

On the other hand, cricket is full of runs. You make them, you get an Audi; you don't, Bishen Singh Bedi's going to sell your '68 Fiat for free. But ask any chess fan what he thinks of the game and he'll give you the same bull about eleven men running around a leather ball for five days for five tests. Know the reason? They think that because there's no pawn to king five or queen's ambit reclined, it must be an unintelligent game. That's why the last batsmen are in and they need one run to win. It's also the last over and here comes the last ball of the rubber.

You get the picture? One vital run needed and the batsman makes an easy shot which could muster three but in the process breaks his leg. (I know this is dumb but let's assume it for the sake of my puzzle.) He's in so much pain that he can't move and there's no substitute runner right then. Question: can they win?

Well, watch this. The striker signals his partner to come over to his end (like in a normal run) while he himself merely extends his bat a couple of inches outside his crease. Then he tells his partner to run back and pulls his bat inside his own crease again. This makes one 'short' run which is not counted (since he hadn't quite made it to the other crease, and one run which is counted — the second one. Schematically so:

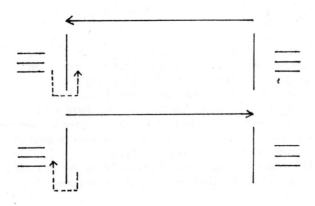

Well? Won or not?

FORUM

I've had conflicting controversial opinions on this one. My friend Kishore Bhimani of much cricket writing fame seems to think that even to accomplish a 'short' run the batsman must have at least crossed half the pitch. However, humble as he is, he told me not to take his word for it but to check up a rules book. Arun Lal (impressed?) thought I was on to a real stumper. All this goes to show that no one seems to know the real answer. But still.

Dear MS,

Suppose a ball is struck by the batsman and both the striker and the nonstriker start for a run, but on seeing a fielder approach the ball, return to their original creases. One run is still scored. The reasoning applied is the same as yours.

The first run is 'short' — the one taken when both move towards the opposite crease, but the second is complete as they have both returned back. An easier way to score runs would be if both the striker and nonstriker hop out and hop back into the crease every time the ball is hit. Obviously this has not caught the cricketers' eyes or else we would have very different matches with little possibility of run outs.

Any comments?

Mohit Nagpal, New Delhi

(*That problem just lay around for several years thinking it had got the better of the cricket association of the world or whoever controls how googlies and things must be bowled during a partial solar eclipse till I met and made belated friends with Dom Moraes and one day while deep into a torporous discourse on the collated plays of Sophocles I let my eyes drift towards his bookshelf and imagine my surprise when I found nestled between a proscenium of feminine endings and a row of Pindaric tetrapody a whole tier of Wisdens.*

"*Hey what's with this cricket shit man?*" *I cut into him mid-sentence on the uses of the waldflute as a polyphonic metaphor.* "*What kind of poet are you anyway?*"

"*I happen to be an expert on the game, Mukul,*" *he replies.* "*Once when Bradman, Sobers and I ...* "

"*Wait a sec,*" *I barged in again,* "*in that case suppose the last batsmen are in and they need one run to ...* "

"*Look, you're looking for a problem for your page, right?*"

"*Actually a solution but go ahead all the same.*"

"*In that case, the bowler bowls, the batsman misses, the ball misses the wicket, the keeper can't collect, the ball keeps travelling, the batsmen start to take a run, but before the nonstriker can make it into the crease a fielder throws in the ball to the wicketkeeper, who then rips off the bails. Got that?*

"*It's in print already.*"

"*So who's out? The striker stumped or the nonstriker run out?*")

58

FORUM

Dear MS,

In the unique cricket problem given, it would have been a bye-run if it would have been completed. However, since it was not, two cases could exist.

Case 1: If the striker has reached the other end before the bails are knocked off, then the nonstriker is run out.

Case 2. If the striker at the other end is also out of the crease, then the fielding team can claim him stumped out or nonstriker run out.

The prerogative lies with the fielding team unlike if the ball would have been hit and a similar situation occurred in which case the prerogative would have lain with the batsmen as to who 'walks' or declares himself out (since this was a genuine stroke).

Howzzat?

Rajesh Mehra, Faridabad

Dear MS,

The rule book clearly states that the striker can be stumped only when he is not going for a run. (See 39.1 of the 1980 code of rules for cricket.)

Yours sportingly,
M Srikant, Bangalore

(Oh, incidentally, the broken legged man's run doesn't count according to some convoluted reasoning Dom gave me after making it up.)

XVI

LOOSE-ROPE WALKER

If the circumference of the earth at the equator is approximately 40,000,000 metres then a rope of that length will just girdle the equator. However, if the rope is only 10 metres longer and if it is somehow held equidistant at all points from the earth, then how big is that gap? The answer's quite surprising. Especially if you consider a man walking around the equator. What extra distance does his head cover compared to the feet?

Waitaminute, don't answer right now. What's the matter with me anyway? How did that no-frills-attached problem spring into being there? Must have been a momentary lapse. Sorry, we'll just have to start all over again.

One generally had nothing to do over the weekend so one went and got all interested in a rope around the earth. These things just happen to lie around in the devil's workshop you know. The point being — if you'll pardon, that is, some mountains and a bunch of ravines, ruts and rents, and gorges, grooves and gullies — that that rope's about a nice fit on the circumference of 40 million metres as she is measured. The point further being that if one still had nothing to do and went and added another ten measly metres (count them) to the twine and then were stupid enough to try and mentally hold it above the surface of our best of all possible terra

firmas equally high everywhere then one would have no choice but to ask how much higher that cerebral rope would be from the interesting one, wouldn't one? One would also be amazed for once. And if one really really even then didn't have anything to do on a perfectly decent weekend otherwise, one could imagine a another one walking around the equator with the head held high and wonder how much more its head headed than its feet footed.

There, isn't that much better?

FORUM

Dear MS,

For 'ones' I thought you had the decency to present a problem in an intelligent manner and I was so 'one' over that I was on the point of solving it when you went and effed it up so badly that now I'm not interested.

Yours uninterestedly,
Hemant Agashe, Chandigarh

Dear MS,

If the radius of the earth is say, R, then the circumference $2\pi R$ = 40,000,000 m. If the length of the rope is 40,000,010 m and at a height 'x' from the surface of the earth then $2\pi(R + x)$ = 40,000,010.

Or, $2\pi R + 2\pi x$ = 40,000,010
Or, 40,000,000 + $2\pi x$ = 40,000,010
Or, $2\pi x$ = 10
Or, x = $10/2\pi$ = $5/\pi$ = 1.59

Therefore the length of the gap is 1.59 m. Similarly, if the man is six feet tall, then his feet will travel a distance of $2\pi R$ and his head a distance of $2\pi (R + 6)$. That is, his head will travel an extra distance of $2\pi \times 6 = 12\pi$ = 37.7 m.

Yours etc,
V Srividya, Madras

XVII

CUE NAHIN?

One droll monsoon, many rains ago, I picked up a Reader's Digestish kind of book called *Be the Person You Want to Be* and, quite ironically, have never been the same since. Not that I had been what I was to begin with, or am now what I might have been had I not been such a fool to have started reading it but still like I said, it was pouring outside and someone had not paid my telephone bill.

The headings of all 16 chapters had the same kind of beginning: 'So You Wanna Be a ... ?' with things like Pilot, Deepsea Diver, Goal-keeper, Cartoonist, Film Director, Commercial Artist, Doctor, and so on and so forth to fill in the blanks. It was exactly all the kind of things I had no intention of wanna ever being. Till I came to 'So You Wanna Be a Billiard Player?' and did a triple take. Who in their right minds, I thought, would especially wanna be a billiard

player? Not counting Wilson Jones and stuff, of course. So naturally that was the chapter I ended up reading first. And after so many years it's paid off in spades.

See, what they did was (to get you all interested in each chapter), they started out with a joke about pilots for instance, or an anecdote about deepsea divers or something amusing that once happened to some goal-keeper and junk. And guess how my chapter began? You got it. With a puzzle. Here it is people.

In billiards the general idea is to topple those balls into the pockets, right? Right; and one way to go about it is to use what is called a 'cue' ball (much like a 'striker' in carrom) to sort of hustle them along on their road to dusty deaths. But tarry. What actually happens is this: as soon as the cue ball hits the other ball the cue ball follows the struck ball a short distance. In fact, it's called a 'follow shot' as opposed to a 'draw shot' where the cue ball returns after the collision. But this shouldn't happen, should it? Because when a moving object hits a stationary object of the same mass, its kinetic energy of the centre of mass is transferred totally. So how's the private dick parody done?

FORUM

Dear MS,

The billiards problem was a stupid one. (*Thanks. The reason was because we hadn't run a stupid answer for a long time — MS*) Anyone with a little knowledge of dynamics, physics and billiards can solve it. (*Meaning like 99 per cent of the population I suppose? — MS*) During a follow shot we hit the cue ball slightly above the centre, while for a draw shot we hit it slightly below the centre. See diagrams (Geet Sethi can vouch for it).

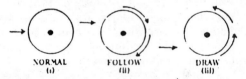

NORMAL   FOLLOW   DRAW
(i)   (ii)   (iii)

In case (i) the only motion is linear. While in cases (ii) and (iii) the ball experiences another force around an axis parallel to the surface, the effect of which is to rotate the ball. After the cue ball has hit the object ball and transferred the linear kinetic energy, this force comes into play. As is obvious from the diagram, for a follow shot it will cause the cue ball to move forward, while from a draw shot it will make the cue ball return. This law is applied to great effect in billiards. Persons like Geet Sethi and I can make the cue ball strike the object ball and come back a much greater distance than it travelled while going forward.

Yours etc,
Rajiv Vasudara, Bombay

XVIII

THE SOUND OF ONE HAND CAPPING

In your deepest sanctums, near where your true heart beats, you've always wanted to hear a dirty joke. I think I've always guessed. Thing is, I know lots, but how does one tie it up with a so-kalled klean kolumn like this without having the culture-vulture hitmen hotting things up for us? Anyway, I've sort of hit upon a kind of solution, viz: base it on some simple physical principle and let fly. So I'd been nursing this one for a long time and now, like some rough beast slouching its way towards Bethlehem, its time has come. (Hang in there literate Christians, no offence meant.)

At the next cocktail party which is inevitably going to be boring your ass off, empty the company paid Scotch bottle's last dregs of offering into your glass and go through the following grind:

"Okay, who wants to scrap whatever junk they're discussing and 'hear' a real filthy one?"

"We! We! We!"

Thus cleared for lift-off, light a match and drop it into the recently emptied bottle. A whoosh of blue flame, full of sound and fury signifying nothing, will leap up and out the neck. Immediately the fireworks are over, clamp the flat of your palm down on the opening and keep it pressed there tightly as you tell the following story:

"Once upon a time there was a king who thought his mate was faithful. Alas, this was lightmiles from the truth. Anyway, one day the king pushed off on one of his holy wars which

64

lasted an incredibly short time as he was a great leader, and before you could exclaim 'infidel' he was back knocking on his bedroom door. His wife thinking she had a solid six months to herself to delect various males was, of course, inside cavorting under the quilt. As her husband entered she performed several doubletakes of 69 in order to hide the accessory after the fact but it was no go. The king, suspecting everything in the world except one, ordered her to come out from under the wraps at once. This the lady immediately did with a sound like ... "

Pause dramatically for a moment here to remove your palm off the bottle top before saying: " ... this."

The question is; what is the simple underlying principle behind the punchline that makes this undeniably one of the filthiest jokes to be found in print without becoming explicitly prurient enough for the anti-porn guys to make their pre-dawn swoop on my hovel?

FORUM

Dear MS,

This is with reference to the anecdote with an unprintable punchline concerning a king, a queen and a quilt.

The simple scientific truth that underlies the case of the quilt is that nature abhors a vacuum — of space, and time as well. And six months is time enough!

Coming to the actual mechanics; the lips of any well-formed bottle, after the disappearance of the old flame, if plugged by any accommodating member (in this case the palm), are quite small and snug so as to enhance mutual attraction and offer resistance to separatist forces. But if the decoupling forces have an upper hand, then it results in those acoustic effects that accompany the forceful entry of heir ... er ... air.

Having laid down the bare facts, let me conclude by saying that the king's holistic approach towards finding the whole, naked truth was quite sound.

Yours sincerely,
J Ashok, Madras

XIX
QUESTIONABLE TAKTIX

You're all familiar with that tremendously popular science quiz programme called 'Quest', right? You know, the one where they have an Einstein team pitted against a Bose team and lots of statistics in between. Well, one of the people who comperes this show is Partho Ghose and he's a great friend of mine even though he doesn't know it as yet.

So what happened was we got together recently to discuss some great things we could do for Indian TV in the interests of those of you who can't sit through yet another meaningless episodic opus made of soap. There we were at the Tolly club, soaking in the sun, slugging back gallons of tomato juice (no beer because January 26th's supposed to be a day of mourning or something) on a crisp holiday morning, when suddenly guess what? Partho starts telling me about some hassles he'd recently had while shooting.

He: Sometimes studio conditions are the pits. Last week I had this super visual conundrum guaranteed to mickey the finn out of both teams, but given the conditions of lighting we got, we just couldn't run the item.

Me: (innocently) Oh gee, that's sad Partho. I grieve for you.

He: Yeah well, that's what life's all about.

Me: I know. Who would have guessed.

He: (in a world of his own) Not any one in the audience either. That's for sure.

Me: (so innocent by now that Central Casting's begun throwing a dragnet for me to star in an update of Rebecca of Sunnybrook Farm) Er, what exactly was the problem?

He: Oh, it was a cute number in the form of a bimetallic strip in a disc configuration which when you rub in front of the audience and keep aside on a table, suddenly goes pop and rockets up towards the ceiling a while later.

Me: (being drug away by Central Casting) And why does this happen?

He: Well see, it's very simple really. For one thing there's really no violation of conservation of momentum as you might believe. For instance, how do you jump? How does a ball bounce? How ...

But by that time I had hightailed it to these keyboards and here it is, a problem with new, improved adjectives for you to grind those bicuspids into. See how much I have to work to entertain you?

FORUM

Dear MS,

When you rub the bimetallic strip (in a disc configuration), the temperature of the strip rises. As a result a thermoelectric potential difference develops along the junction. In the present case the upper surface becomes negative. Now, due to the mutual repulsion of the electric lines of force, the strip will experience a slight concavity. When a light of sufficient intensity is shone on the strip, the electrons escape as photoelectrons and the concavity of the disc disappears. And due to the reaction with the table surface, the disc flies up. (There is, as you say, no violation of the conservation of momentum.)

Most probably the lighting conditions on the Doordarshan sets were not adequate because (if I remember correctly) we need enough light of shorter wavelengths; that is, wavelengths less than that of green light, which was lacking.

Yours etc,
Saswato R Das, Calcutta

XX

OH TO BE AN AQUANUT

The other day I was in the bathtub with a ping pong ball (no I hadn't lost my way; I just find bathing alone boring) and while idly playing with it I found that when I dunked it down to the bottom of the tub and let go, it shot up to the surface and lifted clean out of the water a good two or three inches!

Therefore I've come across this idea. Why not take a rocket — they're airtight anyway — down to the deepest part of the Mariana Trench in the Pacific Ocean and let it go. If it's sufficiently buoyant it should come rocketing up to the surface and might even reach escape velocity and go into orbit. Now you must be thinking that the cost of taking a rocket down to the bottom of the ocean might be prohibitive but I've solved that problem too.

All one has to do is to make that rocket of such material which seawater corrodes rapidly. Now if it is initially heavy enough it can merely be thrown into the water and it will then descend due to its own weight. But while descending, the seawater will be corroding its surface simultaneously. A point will come when it will begin to become buoyant (and this can be engineered so that it happens just when it reaches the bottom) and start to rise. As it rises more of its surface will become eroded thus making it more and more buoyant and thus also increasing its speed till it reaches about seven-and-a-half miles a second.

Then it can go to the moon.

What do you think?

FORUM

Dear MS,

Since you didn't sound too certain whether your ping pong rocket could go to the moon or not, I have discovered a way to make sure it does. Construct a huge paddle of the same material you mentioned and drop it into the ocean first. Then when all the corrosion has taken place and it is on its way up coming faster and faster, drop the rocket. The paddle will swat that stupid rocket clear to the stars.

Have you been bathing with any other kind of balls lately?

Yours sportingly,
Anita Dua, Hyderabad

As a matter of fact, yes Anita. But I could find no problems with them.

XXI

THE IMPAUSEABLE DREAM

Want to know about a poor man's Mukul Sharma in the United States? Read the January 1987 issue of *Discover*. For those of you who can't or (sensibly) won't, his name is either Cecil Adams or Ed Zotti. Meaning they're not only the same person but also phantasms of each other's concoction.

Basically the hustle's like this: Adams/Zotti runs this syndicated column in various newspapers called "The Straight Dope" where he promises to answer readers' questions on any subject under the sun. "All major mysteries of the cosmos succinctly explained," he boasts, boasts *Discover* which then proceeds to give him yards and yards of precious print space — something *India Today* or *Sunday* or *Imprint* or whichever doesn't do for me even though I'm quite obviously much much better. However. Yes, but why do I call him the poor man's MS? Well, mainly because he only has to handle tacklers like: "Are turkeys really so stupid as to look up during rainstorms to see what's happening — and drown?" "Why don't you ever see any baby pigeons?" "Why does chewing spitballs made of aluminum foil

make your teeth hurt?" "Would a glass of water carried into the cold vacuum of space boil or freeze?" "Howcome you can see through glass?" "How did the G-string get its name?" "What is the function of pubic hair?" And so on.

Regarding the last question, incidentally, he does give a beaut of an answer which goes in part: "Various theories have been advanced regarding the purpose of pubic hair. For example, I have a Smithsonian monograph here ... that presents the novel thesis that pubic and axillary (armpit) hair gives babies something to grab on to. My baby does this, it is true, but then she's 29 years old." Now that's genuine Mindsport stuff as you can easily make out.

But here's an example of a question asked which neither Adams/Zotti nor *Discover* could answer: "So often in books and movies, a character will pinch or slap himself when something unbelievable happens, to see if he's dreaming. Have there ever been any cases when someone pinched himself only to suddenly awaken and find he had been dreaming?"

So what's the correct answer? Is it theoretically possible? Actually, I know for a fact that it's even practically possible. How?

FORUM

Dear MS,

This is an answer to can a man in sleep pinch himself and wake up.

Though often such things happen in novels and pictures, it is highly impossible. Normally a sleep pattern consists of two kinds of sleep: REM (Rapid Eye Movement) and NREM (Non-Rapid Eye Movement). About 75 per cent of total sleep is characterized by a gradual deepening reduction in muscle activity. (A little extra: NREM is further divided into four stages with depth of sleep increasing from one to four.) In contrast, REM sleep is associated with fast EEG, *increased body movements (emphasis added — MS)* but still deeper sleep. Thus it is impossible to perform a voluntary act like pinching oneself while asleep. The higher centres responsible for such an act are totally inhibited (ascending reticular system) by the sleep promoting factor called factor S.

Yours faithfully,
Ajit N Patil, Solapur

Sorry to shatter your dreams (so to speak) and wake you up to a reality Ajit (and to all of you who wrote in saying "no" too, though perhaps less eruditely) but here's a bit of information no medical college is going to tell you about. There is a type of dream called a "lucid dream" which approximately one per cent of the population has from time to time. A lucid dream is a dream in which the dreamer realizes

71

that she/he is dreaming and can, with experience, sometimes interfere with and actually change the course of the dream content. Thus, theoretically, the dreamer can even awaken voluntarily. Meaning all a lucid dreamer has to do is dream that she/he is pinching her/his thigh and simultaneously wilfully awaken. British psychologist Celia Green has written an extremely interesting book about this phenomenon called (what else?) Lucid Dreams. *Check in your local library. Alternatively if you still think I'm pulling a real fast one, contact a certain Ms Shohini Ghosh, M-11B, Jangpura Extension, New Delhi 110 014 and find out. She's a lucid dreamer with whom I've personally worked and about whom I've written extensively too.*

So much for Discover *magazine's Ed Zotti being able to answer all questions.*

XXII

A SMALL PARA-DOX

A long time ago — I forget which decade — I ran a massive
scientific gaffe William Golding committed when he said (in
Lord of the Flies) that Piggy's myopic corrective lenses which
are meant for near-sighted people and are concave, were
used as a magnifying lens for lighting a fire. Even the
combined effort of the Doors or Jose Feliciano couldn't light
my fire with that pair of specs. A lot of you people got that
answer so fast, it was embarrassing for a budding Gardner
of the likes of me. But now that I've matured to a Martin,
did you know that Golding went and snafued moments later
in chapter five again? Here's the relevant extract:

> A sliver of moon rose over the horizon, hardly large
> enough to make a path of light even when it sat right
> down on the water; but there were other lights in the
> sky, that moved fast, winked, or went out, though not
> even a faint popping came down from the battle fought
> at ten miles' height. But a sign came down from the
> world of grown-ups, though at that time there was no
> child awake to read it. There was a sudden bright
> explosion and corkscrew trail across the sky; then

darkness again and stars. There was a speck above the island, a figure dropping swiftly beneath a parachute, a figure that hung with dangling limbs. The changing winds of various altitudes took the figure where they would. Then three miles up, the wind steadied and bore it in a great slant across the reef and the lagoon toward the mountain-side, but now there was a gentle breeze at this height too and the parachute flopped and banged and pulled. So the figure with feet that dragged behind it, slid up the mountain. Yard by yard, puff by puff, the breeze hauled the figure through the blue flowers, over the boulders and red stones, till it lay huddled among the shattered rocks of the mountain-top.

There's an absolutely horrible scientific mistake Golding's made somewhere up there. Defy you to find it. Defy you also to find out where I got that one from.

FORUM

Dear MS,

To begin with, the parachute cannot, on account of its construction, slide up the mountain side. A parachute has a hole at the top which is responsible for the dynamics which help the parachute to smoothly settle down. One can be dragged by a parachute over plain land, but a parachute can never slide up a mountain side. Or else Hillary and his associates wouldn't have taken that many days to stagger up the Everest. Instead they could have hooked on a para and...

Yours insincerely,
Navin Dutt, Ozhar
Township (HAL)

Fast work is correct. Faster work is dead wrong. The hole(s) on top of a parachute are not large enough to retard the accumulation of air inside the canopy. One could very easily be dragged up a mountain side. And, for your information Navin D, Hillary and his cronies staggered up 29,002 feet because that was the point, going it on your own. By your logic they could have also used a helicopter.

74

Dear MS,

This refers to your quotation from Golding's *Lord of the Flies*, which incidentally was originally published in *Puzzles From Other Worlds*. (*Thanks a lot for going public!* — MS)

The mistake Golding made was that he described the moon rising just after sunset, as a "sliver of moon". Under such conditions, it can only be a full moon. While you had included the quotation which mentions that a "sliver of moon rose over the horizon", you had left out the preceding paragraph which mentions "The day had just ended". Hence your puzzle was really incomplete and meaningless.

V Chandran, Bombay

Oooooops!

XXIII
DIFFERENT BALL GAME

Know what a superball is? It's something the United States has given to the rest of the world besides the comic strip and Norman Mailer. You can buy it off the shelf in that country and bring it home to amaze friends and mothers-in-law. Actually it's just a hard packed rubber ball which bounces much more on the rebound than most balls do, that's all. But it's great fun.

Because for one thing, once you've set it in motion by hurling it across your expensive living room, you can be sure some pretty fine porcelain is going to go to pieces as you watch with dull, uncomprehending eyes.

Anyway, the point I was trying to make is that the same effect can be achieved with an old golf ball too. What effect? Coming to that in a sec. I assume you don't have a superball. But you can lay your phalanges on a discarded tee-off. Just bore a hole on the surface of one such and insert a pencil (pointy edge in).

Then drop the structure — pencil side up — on the floor. Guess what happens? The pencil rockets away at a speed close to dazzle your id. If instead of a pencil you use sticks of varying length, you'll be sure to find a length which, when inserted into the hole and dropped, will not make the ball

bounce at all! You'll hear a dull thud as the ball makes an off-Broadway entrance and stays put while the stick rockets off at random. In fact, that's the catch. Make damn sure that the ball lands with the stick pointing directly upwards or it's going to be instant nightblindness for someone in that gaping crowd.

And to conclude it all, here's a rider. Take an ordinary football; put an ordinary tennis ball on top of it and drop the duo in tandem vertically.

Write in with results.

FORUM

(Ideally, given the perfect lighting conditions, this is how I work. I set a problem in P-K4 and then, since I neither have the time nor brains to solve them (the hard ones, that is) I wait for someone to write in the right answer. When it finally comes in I file it and wait for four weeks and run them and wait for my world to blow up around me if it's wrong. Guess what happened to the file containing the answer to this one? Yup, I lost it. Naturally I couldn't say that in print and thereby admit I didn't know the answer either. So I sat tight. Whenever someone would write in to inquire about the answer, I'd quietly tear up the letter. Don't tell me; I know I'm terrible. Anyway the point is, since I've made a clean breast of it, is anybody still interested in writing in the answer? Promise to run it in Second Worst of Mindsport.*)*

XXIV

SCIENCE FRICTION

Picked up a lousy book the other day called *The Science in Science Fiction: Does Science Fiction Foretell the Future?* The premise of the book, from the cover on, is biased and pig-headed. Just look at the naive and crass presumption. Whoever said that SF is supposed to foretell the future? It's like adopting a premise: Do Crime Thrillers Demystify Crime, and then, after proving that they do not, chucking the body out with the bathwater.

That's exactly what Messrs Lang and Stableford have done. Having conclusively proved beyond the shadow of any doubt that SF does not in any way foretell the future, they have relegated this marvellous genre to less than gutter-pulp level. Of course, in the process they have also made an ass of themselves, considering that Arthur C Clarke predicted the communication satellite way way back in 1945 when even Telstar couldn't be spelt correctly by non-existent NASA personnel without gagging.

However, it is true that SF sometimes does get it wrong, but then that's not SF's fault. H G Wells wasn't supposed to know that relativity was around the corner when he wrote *The First Men on the Moon*. And that one of the general theory's consequences is that there's no way by which one can insulate against gravity. Wells, in fact, seems to be a favourite whipping boy of these authors.

"So Wells's invisibility," they write, "is convincing at first reading. It is unlikely though, that a man's blood could be decolourized without killing him; it is even more unlikely that the retina of each eye should remain visible after the process. If the retinas were invisible, light would pass through them without effect and the invisible man would be blind."

Old hands will probably remember that we had run this same problem earlier and had received a beauty of a rejoinder by one A K Jain who had written in saying that the invisible man would not necessarily be blind because "visible" light (or more correctly what our so-called associational areas of the neocortex interpret photo-chemical activation of a light receptive pigment and the primary excitation-initiating process as the subjective sensation of "vision") is only a small part of the entire electromagnetic spectrum. Thus, theoretically, it is possible for a man to have retinas which are transparent to this visible band while remaining opaque to the rest, or part thereof, of it. Such a man would remain invisible to us, yet at the same time be able to, according to Jain, "see" in the ultraviolet or infrared or whatever.

For example do bees "see" polarized light? Do pigeons "see" geomagnetism? Is our pineal gland "seeing" light when it gets triggered by it to start functioning as an inhibitor in the growth of the gonads?

Anyway, to return to the book, I must say I picked up a little gem of an error made by Charles Eric Maine in *High Vacuum* where his spacesuited characters cannot hear the sound of their own footsteps because "sound cannot travel in a vacuum".

What mistake did Maine make?

FORUM

Dear MS,

With reference to the sound of footsteps in vacuum, I think Charles Eric Maine should have said "sound cannot exist in a vacuum," rather than "sound cannot travel in a vacuum." Right? (*Wrong* — MS)

Yours etc,
Dev Kumar Vasudevan,
Mhow

79

Dear MS,

I thoroughly enjoy reading the racy humour of your column. In fact, Mindsport is the first thing I read in the *Illustrated Weekly* (*Now you know why we're running your wrong letter, don't you?* — *MS*)

Well, the reason why the astronaut (in Maine's mistake) cannot hear the sound of his footsteps is simply because there is no sound. He doesn't walk in outer space as he does on earth, but only floats around because there is no gravity. (*Not even of the situation?* — *MS*) So the fact that sound cannot travel in a vacuum is immaterial.

> Yours admiringly,
> Vatsala Subramaniam,
> Coimbatore

Dear MS,

Spacemen can hear their footsteps because solids (for instance, shoes) can transmit sound to their ears via the air inside their suits, a la stethoscopes. (*Actually, it is the bones that would be more efficient, and faster, in transmitting the sound* — *MS*)

> Yours etc,
> L A Ramanathan, Mysore

XXV

KIN-FLICKS

I'm going to stick my neck out so far this time that I suspect Lamarckism is going to stage a comeback. Complete with Lysenko riding a giraffe. Never mind if that passed over your head at Mach 4. Never mind it that too honeyed a tachyon across your mind. (Boy, am I having fun! Like my friend Vithal Nadkarni is fond of saying: "Hey, you've got a laid back style there Mukul." And I go "Heh, heh, heh. I dream of Dixieland every day, didn't you know?")

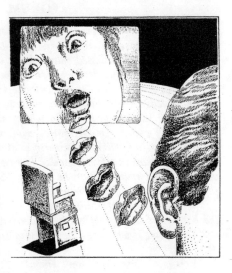

To come back to the English language for better communication, the reason for my stretching the isthmus between the cranium and its carcass is because I have this *deja vu* I've run this before in my previous life when I used to see a lot of movies at movie theatres and not on a 1.7 inch back-lit gas plasma diagonal. I remember I had a girl friend called Bernadette (who is now much married and many offsprung, thank you, and will automatically deny the entire torrid fugue as a figment of her teenage imagination) who would insist on watching horror films so she could use the climax scenes as an excuse to hold hands in that sweaty aisle side corner seat in back of the hall.

It was during the monitoring of a spooky called *Wait Until Dark* (yes, that's how old I am) that this problem first entered my head and ignited my skullcap. Okay, I thought, so we're sitting at the back of the auditorium. And way, way up ahead a lot of people are sitting at shotgun distance in the front row. Now light travels at 300,000 km per second. That means the visual component of Audrey Hepburn reaches me at almost the same time at it reaches the loafers in front. Or, at least, the difference in time must be in the order of an atto. However, sound travels at 344 metres per second in air at 20 degrees C. If a movie theatre is 50 metres from the screen to the lovers' row at the back then Ms Hepburn's speech should take approximately .14 seconds to arrive after her image, right?

Lip synchronization would obviously suffer. So how is this problem overcome by the likes of Yippee it's Dipy or G P or whatever Sippy and gang?

FORUM

(This one got no takers from the audience and I let it ride for years thinking what the hell, who cares, now that we don't even visit those rat and cockroach infested movie halls any more and decimal point differences in lip-sync don't matter so long as you can move the chair up as close as you want to the cathode ray gizmo. But as a seeker of pure knowledge, truth, and beauty on that eightfold path of enlightenment the problem still nagged me. So while compiling this selection I rang up this guy called Amit Khanna who makes films in his sleep and knows things like why the universe exists and asked him what gives.

"Call me back in a few seconds," he says and while I'm just beginning to hit that old redial button he replies, "Sorry, but apparently that's a problem that just, well, remains."

"What do mean remains," I say. "What about huge big halls where the back rows are a football field away. What then?"

"Well that's why they have individual headsets or speakers in drive-ins."

"You mean even you don't know?"

"Of course I do. Didn't I just tell you that I know that there's no solution to the problem?'

"Okay then why does the universe exist?")

XXVI

SWEDE SIXTY

This is just in case you thought I know next to nothing about politics and other things like that that go on behind my back when I'm not looking. It should also put *The Hindu* to shame for not having come up with this solution to what will haunt poor Arun Shourie till the evening of his life or morning, whichever comes later.

An inventor offers a large new gun to a government, appointed committee on the verge of making a fast buck by calling it everything except a bribe. The guy says that, once loaded, his gun can fire 60 shots at the rate of a shot a minute. The committee passes the buck to the army who put it to the test and find that it fires 60 shots an hour. The committee declines to buy the gun (this is not reality, remember?) on the grounds that it does not fulfil the promised condition.

"Hey wait a minute," says the inventor, "it does exactly what I said it would."

"No way," reply the experts. "It does nothing of the kind. We're not buying."

So who's right? The Before and After man or the science fiction committee? Or who?

FORUM

Dear MS,

Why are you bent on insulting my intelligence? Even a five-year-old will tell you that a shot a minute is exactly the same as sixty shots an hour. (60 minutes = one hour, in case you've forgotten.)

Yours truly,
Kapil Mehta, IIT-Delhi

Thank you KM. It isn't everyday one gets such startling information. But just in case you're interested in the answer, gaze upon the following.

Dear MS,

Regarding the puzzle about the gun and gunshots, the experts were correct. As per the inventor the gun fired 60 shots at the rate of one a minute. Hence, as the first shot is fired, the clock measuring the time taken for firing is also started. If the next shot is fired after a minute and so on, 60 shots will be fired in 59 minutes. The catch is that the time duration of the firing is measured from the first shot. Thus the gun had failed.

Yours faithfully,
Amit Sharma, Bangalore

XXVII
FINER THAN PRINT

I always thought these kind of things happened only in O
Henry short stories. A friend's uncle recently lost out on a
huge loot of lolly. Apparently there was this big contest with
the usual first prize for two to Singapore or some such other
supermarket if you could identify the six sportsmen and
associate them with the alongside pix of bats or racquets or
paddles or oars or gloves or steroids and then complete a
sentence beginning "Super champs love Superchump Chomps
because ... " in 1350 words or less and our hero overcreated
a slogan so original that even before the ink had dried he
was packing his toothbrush around his socks.

But Jesus, Allah, Krishna (in case the cultists' hit brigade
decides to turn me into waffles with maple syrup and Rushdie),
come the day of the full page result announcement and who
should get it but some unnecessary typist from Bagdogra with
a name to match and a slogan Ogilvy or Benson would have
mixed with catfood to feed their goldfish. Anguish writ large
on his papyrus lined forehead our hero complained only to
be told that though his was the masterpiece for the ad club
hall of fame he was disqualified because he was a relative of
someone who worked for the agency handling the Superchump
account. And that it was clearly there in the fine print.

This is a true story because I saw the fine p in question and, yea, even with my 20/20 ophthalmic equipment all I could see were some grey specks of dust arranged in neat rows at the bottom of the page. Clearly, a magnification with a quantum tunnelling device was required.

But enough of faffing already. Here's the problem.

Given no artificial aid whatsoever such as a magnifying glass, spectacles, curved glass-bowls full of water, etc, is there any other way one can still manage to read fine print which appears otherwise as a blur to the unaided eye? There is. It depends on a common phenomenon in physics.

FORUM

Dear MS,

Only your asinine attitude of publishing unconvincing answers prompts me to write an answer for your magnifying stuff. How about using a gravitational lens? Because it is impossible otherwise to enlarge without any accoutrement.

Yours etc,
R Swaminathan, Madras

On the contrary it is not. Too bad RS of M has never heard of the pin-hole camera. Or the diffraction of light. Now listen to the real explanation. Then weep, my children.

Dear MS,

Regarding the question about reading fine print without any aid: I think it can be done if you saw through your fingers. That is, through the space between your fingers when they are kept close together. Or any slit-like structure. At least I could.

Yours truly,
Indraneil Dasgupta, Bombay

Dear MS,

Keep the fine print on a horizontal surface and look at the letters from a distance about equal to the length of your nose and you will see the unseeable. A half formed tear drop forms a natural lens.

Yours etc,
Anil Kumar, Hisar

XXVIII

PARA KEATS

Remember Keats's "Ode To A Nightingale"? Well, here's some background dope on how the poet arrived at one of the finest tributes to this singing sensation. In the words of Charles Brown with whom Keats was living at the time of penning the poem: "In the spring of 1819, a nightingale had built her nest near my house. Keats felt a tranquil and continual joy in her song; and one morning he took his chair from the breakfast table to the grass plot under a plum tree,

where he sat for two or three hours. When he came into the house, I perceived he had some scraps of paper in his hand, and these he was quietly thrusting behind the books. On inquiry I found these scraps, four or five in number, contained his poetic feeling on the song of our nightingale."

Notice anything wrong here? Even if you don't, don't worry; you're in good company. Neither did Sophocles, Shakespeare, or T S Elliot.

FORUM

Dear MS,

Keats and Shakespeare may have been terrific versifiers but were obviously poor aviarists. When they heard a nightingale croon they should have lifted its wings and scrutinized its sex closely. Contrary to popular belief, it is the male nightingale which is a tuneful, soulful warbler. Its song is a courtship melody to attract his mate which, alas, remains superciliously unmusical and silent. Contrary to another popular belief, nightingales sing during day and night — the males that is — and generally between mid-April and mid-June, when Cupid strikes.

Yours etc,
Aarti Raina, Srinagar

XXIX
NO IDLE BOSE

I was meeting Bhaskar after many years. Some idea of the longevity of the interval can be gauged if you realize that the last time I met him he was a janitor with DCPL; today he heads the typing pool. Anyway, he was over the other day, stinking of qwerty and gassing about some turn-key project he was keyboarding in Kenya when I had to stop him short. Wiping away a rind of stray froth still foaming in enthusiasm about his sign-language lips, he asked me if I wanted a fresh problem.

By some strange paranormal quirk of fate, I found myself suddenly grovelling at his feet, saying brokenly, "Yes, yes please, but don't breathe a word of this to Douglas Hofstadter."

"Did you know," he began, "that once upon a time there was a sage who lived only several hundred yards away from a river?"

"No," I drooled on the floor, "tell me more."

"Well, consider a river bank to begin with," he said. And what passes below as an illustration is my "consideration".

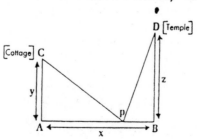

"Mark two points on the bank," he went on, "as A and B such that the distance AB is, say, x. Perpendicularly up from A, at a distance y is C which is the short form of the cottage of said sage. And ditto up from B at a distance z is D which is a temple where the sage and the all-knowing deity rap daily."

"Where's the problem?" I panted, grabbing his hand and giving the back of the wrist a heartfelt kiss.

"The point is that the sage has to ablute (*Look it up* — MS) himself first. Only after laving (*Lay it again, slam* — MS) can he live it up with the loving Lord. The problem is, which is the point P along AB which will yield the shortest distance for CP + PD?"

More deflated than defeated, I began, "But Bose, all those fou -year-old high school kids and 32-year-old IIT chaps will make *keema* curry out of this."

"No way," he says. "Who wants geometry? I'm asking for an elegant, commonsense solution which is staring you in the eye."

Dotbust him, you AK-47 licensed gunrunners.

FORUM

Dear MS,

Though a medico by choice I still remember my basic physics. So here I wish to help your sage find the shortest path by the simplest method.

1. Get a mirror from a female devotee (females need that even if they are not in worldly matters any more) (*Naturally, because they're better looking than males* — MS).

2. Place it on the river bank in between AB such that

3. a torch kept at C at night will be seen reflected at temple D in the mirror.

4. At this stage angle of incidence = angle of reflection which is, of course, the shortest path a light ray takes!

Yours,
S V Prabhu, Bombay

PS: 5. If a mirror is not available use a crow for a torch and food for mirror.

XXX
COAT UNCOAT

(The beautiful women who regularly look after this page hassle me no end for headings. Therefore I decided to start with one this time which has no relevance to the text whatsoever. Bite the dust sylphs.)

Two weeks? three weeks? I don't remember, but a lately whiles ago I and Binita suddenly decided to look up a friend called Rita who graces the Air-Indian skies and naturally smuggles T-shirts out for me through the green or red or amber or whatever channel they have for psychotropic underwear and found to my delight that a planchette was in progress. The works, you know. Complete with dim lights, thick smoke and the Paul Butterfield Blues Band yodelling forgotten Baby Boomer numbers while the four-on-the-floor arched themselves around a pencil trapped between the index and middle above a derelict sheet of paper with A to Zee across the top and the beginnings of the decimal system below. But alas, they rued, "He cometh not and neither the graphite glideth."

Enter the moving finger.

"People, people," I wailed in distraught consternation, "you know not how the very spirits will be summoned."

"Master, master," they hailed in humble unison, "show us!"

Whereupon I did beseech suchlike: "Bring me as you would an emptied glass of wine and unto you I will produce anon those same keening of wraiths that is your deep soul's desire."

However, to cut the BS short, as soon as the required stemware (Sw) was brought I appropriated an air to myself that was most becoming for the lore of spectres and thereupon thence instantly cleansed my hands with soap and water (hint, hint).

(Actually, since Kavita and Meher insist on the *Weekly's* unwritten but fading ground rules regarding relevance of heading to text, is it possible to take off one's shirt without removing one's coat?)

Having thusly scoured mine phalanges I proceeded as follows. About the slightly wetted rim of the Sw I laid the fleshly section of my forefinger and made the same circumnavigate the lip time and again and again till — 'struth — a mournful ululation did emerge and fill the room with tremor and disquietude. Ere I knew, sounds of "Alack!" rent the spheres.

Try it sometime. It's great for faking seances. But let's know why that sound is produced. And no big chill out.

FORUM

Dear MS,

Kavita and Meher could have told you how to remove your shirt without removing your coat. We women do it all the time. Not remove your shirt, that is, but as a parallel, remove our bras without removing the nightie or the blouse. This presumes, of course, that either the overcoat is loose or the undercoat is stretchable, or both.

To uncoat:

1. Unbutton undercoat, be it shirt or bra (it does not matter if the buttons are in front or at the back).

2. Wriggle, pull and stretch one side of undercoat from under the overcoat and off the arm (immaterial if the overcoat has buttons or not). Any arm first.

3. Do likewise to the other side of the undercoat. At this stage you will have an undercoat stretched horizontally from armholes or sleeves.

4. Pull at any of the two sides, and gradually pull the entire undercoat out from under the overcoat.
Good luck.

Anee Takers, 2/1/1 Bright Street, Palm House, Calcutta

Dear MS,

There was no need for the hint. The species of sound produced is the same as what you get when you shampoo your hair "squeeky" clean or rub the bow across the strings of a violin. Discrete units of sound when run together produce a continuous tone. The finger does not run smoothly over the rim of the glass but in a series of jerky interrupted movements with each jerk-stop producing one unit of sound.

The acoustics of the glass do the rest. Not washing the hands would result in a thin film of grease which would make the finger slide without stops and thus produce no sound.

Thusly yours,
David Sassoon, Burnpur

XXXI
RATHER-IN-LAW

Know something? Lewis Carroll's in good company. He too used to write a Mindsport-like column in *The Monthly Packet* from April 1880 onwards for a number of years. In Carroll's own words: "The ... intention ... was to embody in each ... one or more mathematical questions — in arithmetic, algebra or geometry, as the case might be — for the amusement,

and possible edification, of the fair readers of that magazine."

And guess what else? He also used to get a lot of mail, although nothing remotely approaching our cache. Thus, I was vastly relieved to discover that at least in that one department we were streets ahead. (Meaning, so will you kindly not discontinue the barrage?) In the mean time here's an eg of something you'd have been trying to solve in case your great great grandmother had produced you instead of producing your great grandmother.

The Governor of Kgovjni (writes Carroll in his column) wants to give a very small dinner party, and invites his father's brother-in-law, his brother's father-in-law, his father-in-law's brother and his brother-in-law's father. Find the number of guests.

Ten answers (continues Carroll pathetically and we mourn with him) have been received. Of these, one is wrong. Galanthus Nivalis Major, who insists on inviting only two guests — one being the Governor's wife's brother's father. If she had taken his sister's husband's father instead, she would have found it possible to arrive at the correct answer.

Of the nine who send right answers, Sea Breeze (obviously, they used more creative pseudonyms then compared to our hideous "Anon"s now) is the very faintest breath that ever bore the name! "Wind of the western sea", you have had a very narrow escape! Be thankful to appear in the class list at all! Bog-Oak and Bradshaw Of The Future use genealogies which require 16 people instead of 14. Caius and Valentine deserve special mention as the only two who have supplied correct genealogies.

Now although the above (this is me now) is absolutely authentic text, I have deleted certain small portions and have quite cleverly, I believe, changed the structure of a few sentences in order not to reveal the answer. However, a lot of clues still exist in the mainframe for you to chew on and solve this one-hundred-year-old problem.

In fact, I'll give away the one clue you really need. I've inserted a particular word without which half your problem would have been solved.

And that's another clue!

FORUM

Dear MS,

The Governor of Kgovjni must have been named Kanjoos. He invited just one lousy guest to dinner. And what an inbreeding clan! The guest was the Guv'nor's father's sister's husband; whose daughter was spliced to the Guv'nor's brother; whose brother's daughter the Gov himself walked the aisle with; whose son's troth was plighted to the Gov'nor's sister — a sort of coupling in reverse and I don't mean to be vulgar.

Yours blah blah blah,
K Venkatesh, New Delhi

I don't think that's correct but it's too convoluted to figure out. Besides, why must we always have all the right answers? It's only from our mistakes that we ultimately learn, don't we? Otherwise life would be so drab, no? Or what? In the meantime I've got to have a word with young Baiju Parthan.

(*Actually this wasn't the first time someone caught a clue from Baiju's illustration. That Parthan thinks that just because he's the greatest illustrator that side of the Suez he can take pity on readers on this side and donate answers.*)

XXXII

ONE A PENNY, THREE A PENNY

The other day a friend of mine who specializes in reading everything in the *Weekly* except this column told me why he didn't. Read this column, that is. Actually he needn't have bothered because I already knew: either he loved politics or he couldn't solve problems, which, come to think of it, is the same thing. However, the reason he gave me was different. He said he didn't read it was because he could write it! Never one to pass up an opportunity knocking itself stupid on the stoop I (innocently) asked him what problem he would run, say, in a hypothetical MS were he to ever think of coup d'etating me and he replied that he had this one puzzle tucked away in his pancreas for a long time and that that was what he would start with.

Then he bared his little black sweetbread to me.

Seems like the 50 paise (paisa?) coin we use to lull beggars into believing they're for free is either an inch or 2.5 centimetres in diameter. (In reality 2.5 cm works out to .9842525 inches but what the hell; what are friends for?) Now let's visualize a 50 paisa (paise?) outfit where the radius is exactly one inch. Obviously, if we had several such coins and we lined them up in a row we would be able to measure off distances in even numbers like two, four, six, eight and so on inches. The question is, using a number of these same coins, set up in any way, can odd numbered distances also be measured?

On second thoughts this is a very easy one but so much has already been written and I have to take the kids to the zoo now to frighten the animals that we'll let it ride. Promise to give an easier one next time.

FORUM

Dear MS,

I have tried everything in my power to stop your silly page but nothing seems to work. I have even written to the editor and publisher Mr Nandy but have not heard from him till now. It seems I may have to ultimately write to the owners themselves (*Try writing to the vice-president of Mexico; I'm told he has quite a hold on me — MS*) so that the youth of India are not further corrupted by your lies, lies and lies. You are a bloody fool because you take all your problems from other men's books (*Not true. I once took a problem from* The Collected Works of Nalini Jaywant — *MS*) and pass them on as your own. Even your readers are bloody fools for not reading our holy books but reading your bloody shit. This is your last chance or I will have to use stronger methods.

Go to hell.

Sujit Deb

Notice something? People who think they're using dirty words or making threats never give their address. But from the inland I could make out it was from Dhanbad. If any of you good coalminers know the guy, lam him one for me too. Thanks. Meanwhile, lets get back to the Rig Veda.

Dear MS,

Hi! Your fans apart, thru your column, even I have formed a micro fan following of mine. It's at their instance I'm writing this. Why not do yourself a favour — PRINT IT! (*OKAY! — MS*)

Yes, odd numbered distances, too, can be measured.

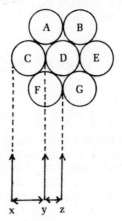

Join the intersecting/touching points of coins A & B to C,D & E and F & G. xy is now three inches and zy is one inch.

Thanking you,
Vivek Jain, Baroda

XXXIII

GO MANGO

First they came in through the mail; then some of them got hold of my number; and now — as if night terrors will never cease — they've found out where I park my carriage from sunup to moonshine five-and-one-half days of the week, months on end, year after sombre, lacklustre year and so on. Conjecture then, if you will, my complete surprise the other day when a nice lady called Shehnaaz Rajen who has conceded a good part of her life in helping me understand the nature of reality tells me there's a someone who wishes to see me just for the heck of it. "Can't be," I say but she goes on regardless. "He says he only wants to find out if you're the same person who writes Mindsport." "Okay," I find myself

vocalizing in gloom, trying to figure out how I can be another guy when I'm already I, "but frisk him for firearms first."

Turns out he's harmless until — hold your breath — he produces from his dreary deeps his dark design: an Endgame! "I have come all this way," he informs me sinisterly, "to give you an Endgame." So I've judged him wrong. He isn't about to do a hatchet job on me after all. He's got a problem for me, man. Goes like this:

There's these two kids out to make a killing in the mango mart. Rustling up the required fruits of labour they figure the most decent thing to do would be to sell 30 a day considering that sort of puts them in business for a month. So much is comprehensible using only transactional analysis. It's the next part which blurs into

101

ontology because kid A sells his *Mangifera indicas* @ two for five paise while B pitches them at three for ditto p. Thusly, A makes 75p at the end of the day while our hero can only shore up a trifling 50p. However, a hefty Rs 1.25 together. Nice and all. Then tragedy strikes. Kid A dies a horrible death at the hands of a serious Reaganomist, leaving a grief-stricken B to double duty for old times' sake. Not heavy into dual personality research, B hunkers down to the job in a burst of brilliance by selling three plus two equals five of the drupes for five plus five equals ten p. At this point mathematics raises its ugly head for figures because the pull at the end of the day turns out to be 60 juicies at five for ten p equals Rs 1.20! O horror horror horror; where alack, is that renegade two bit 5p gone to?

And this he wants me to run as Endgame I ask him? This novella? Doesn't he know that readers, by the time they reach Endgame, are so desperately tired of being amazed, they can take in nothing more than a sentence or two of a problem? In fact, they read it first.

"So pawn it to king four," he says.

So I did.

FORUM

An amazing thing has happened. For the first time in recorded history a puzzle-setter has set a problem and everybody has solved it! How was I supposed to know that all the people in the world knew what the answer was? Or that every alternate one of them would start writing in immediately. Okay you can stop because I can take a hint — that there's no need to publish the answer. I should be given a prize or something.

(Actually so much mail had come in in response to this problem that there really was no point in publishing the answer. But the point is, I still don't know what happens to the 5p. Since you've already shelled out so much cash for this book will someone please cough out another bit for a postcard and inform ours truly?)

XXXIV

SCREAM OF CONSCIOUSNESS

One reader has written in saying that the trouble with me is that I take a really dumb little problem which any grade school kid can solve and then present it as an experimental stream of consciousness novel — a la Shawn and Shem as they wake beside the riverrun past bend of bay at Liffey's to wielderfight their penisolate ... damn! there I go again. Yes, well, that quite accurately put, is my problem.

But I've figured out a natty way to get out of the hassle. What I'll do this time instead is take a really dumb little problem which not only any grade school kid can solve, but present it in such a way that they could even read and understand it. Fair enough?

Below are two identical screws placed together exactly as shown in the illustration. Turn the upper screw in the direction as indicated

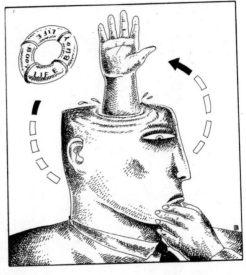

by the arrow and turn the lower one as shown by the lower arrow. Will the two heads of the screws get nearer or further apart? (In case you're thinking who cares, join the club.)

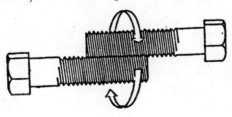

There, I did it. Gave you a paragraph of the dullest prose ever to grace these pages. Hope you're happy trying to solve this idiotic oldie. Meanwhile, if you'll pardon me, I have to go to some crowded place and throw up in public.

FORUM

Dear MS,

Your bolts problem (pinched from Martin Gardner) (*No, from Scot Morris — MS*) reminded me of a problem I heard recently. A lawn sprinkler rotates in a clockwise direction. What direction will it rotate if immersed upside-down in a bucket of water after its hose is connected to the inlet of a pump?

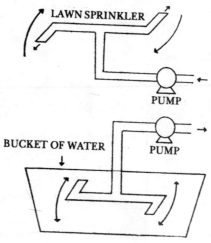

Sincerely yours,
A Misra, Calcutta

Dear MS,

A Misra's lawn sprinkler problem, at least according to me, yields to the following bit of reasoning. First consider the situation where water is being expelled. As long as the water emanates radially from the centre of the sprinkler, it has no angular momentum about the centre. The moment it turns the bends in the arms of the sprinkler the water acquires angular momentum about the centre. To conserve angular momentum, the sprinkler turns anticlockwise (that is, if the water is being emitted clockwise) as in figure (A).

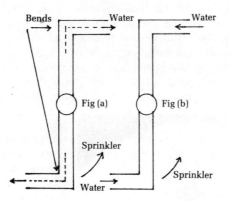

On the other hand, when water is sucked in it initially has angular momentum about the centre but rounding the bends in the arms destroys this, so that the angular momentum is imparted to the sprinkler which still rotates anticlockwise as in figure (B).

Yours etc,
Vishwambhar Pati, Bangalore

Damn good. Clap clap clap and all that. Nice to see you guys go off on your own little trip and have a lot of fun. But what happened to my original problem? My shiny new problem.
(Nobody's answered so far.)

XXXV
SCHOOL ZOUT

Apparently being a father means I'm supposed to help with my daughters' homework from time to time. I look forward to these sessions because we invariably end up arguing about the merits and demerits of the westernized education system as opposed to the *guru-shishya* mode of imparting wisdom. I particularly like to single out the examination infrastructure to vent my wrath on because I tell them it's nothing more than just a test of how well one can cheat from memory.

Of course, needless to say, their teachers and my relatives, friends and spouses frown on this kind of rap, thinking that I should instead be more fruitfully wasting my time teaching them absurd things like how the cold Labrador current meets the warm Gulfstream current which causes fogs in Newfoundland so that it is the second largest exporter of codfish to the Cayman Islands. Or, how Qutb-ud-Din Mubarak the slave king lost the second battle of Panipat to Shah Alam II so that Warren Hasting's tomb could be looted. Or, how zinc peroxide is the main catalyst in the extraction of silica gel so that the nitrogen cycle gets immediately replaced. You get the drift? And of course my kids just lap it up.

So I was mildly surprised the other day when one of them interrupted me while I was babbling about how even if the two sides of a triangle are congruent then the angles opposite to these sides being also congruent makes no difference to anyone in their right senses.

106

"But teacher says that if you have to prove it you have to construct an altitude which divides the triangle into symmetrical halves," she said.

"Tell her to go jump," I retorted, making sure no one was listening. "It can also be proved using no construction at all. Isn't that an easier way to get rid of that theorem forever?"

She yelped in glee when I explained how.

FORUM

Using trig erotica like a/sin A = b/sin B = c/sin C is a no-no. You either geometry it or forget it. The way to prove the base angles of an isoceles triangle equal without using any construction was first demonstrated by the geometer Pappus around AD 300 who showed that in the triangle.

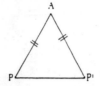

since AP and AP1 are of equal length, therefore triangles PAP1 and P1AP are congruent. This implies that corresponding angles are equal. In particular, the two base angles are equal.

Then in 1960, a computer program designed to find proofs of theorems in elementary Euclidean geometry also hit upon something similar. It considered the triangle and its mirror image as two different triangles. Then having proved them congruent, it pointed out that the two base angles matched each other in this congruence. This is supposed to be one of the first and finest examples of computer originality. Matched only by Shojan K Joseph, S Jhunjhunwala, Pankaj Gupta, Saswato Ranjan Das, Ajith K Narayan and Vinay V so far.

LOST IT AT THE FLICKS

Now it can be told. Now that Prakash Nadkarni has migrated to the United States, it can, like I, just said, be, tol, d. If I have ever met my match as a jack of all tirades, it was Prakash. The rat knew all about everything even though he was a pharmacist. You name the subject and that fink would know about it. In the short spell of what was it? about a year or so maybe at the outside perhaps, if that, I must of sprung macroeconomics, monotremata (look it up), myeloblastemia (look it up), magnetic resonance imaging (look it up), metempsychosis (look it up), motorcycle maintenance (read it up) and on one desperate occasion even Mindsport to that reptile and the slime would end up pitching me a bull session that made me feel like a dab of Mobil on highway 66 revisited. **Know what I mean?** It's okay, I neither.

However, this is how I plan to get back at him in my own venal, unscrupulous way. Because he's not around these parts no more I'm going to make up a story which almost never happened that will make the grey cells in his brain squirm into a darker shade of pale.

See, I had once called him over for dinner, and, knowing my penchant and sun sine for hogging those old footlights and swaying in the ladies only department, I sneakily asked him the day before if he knew anything about the French post-Restoration comedy of manners and was enchanted to see his jaw drop beneath my wisdom like a stone. "Well then that's all we're going to talk about on the morrow's eve, dear and beloved Adam," I smirked in a burst of disdain bordering on sin and left him a shambling psychological cripple. But hear this.

Knowing also that he'd have rewritten the biography of Racine and Moliere overnight, when the time came and we were surrounded 'neath the smoggy skies by gaggles of neglected nymphets, I volleyed off my first salvo by asking him if he had seen the *nouvelle vague* film *Fils de Put* made by none other than Greek *cinema verite's enfant terrible* Doric "The Ionic" Corinthian. After the gentle ladies with the lamp had bandaged his mandible back to his mouth I casually inquired if in that film he remembered the grand banquet scene wherein we had a dining room with one wall fully covered by a huge mirror and that at one point a shot was taken showing the diners as a reflection in it from an angle directly in front of the mirror. So howcome, I asked — the Mohammed Ali kayo looming up at last — the reflection of the camera was not seen in the mirror?

And no smartass answers please because this is not a trick question. The camera angle is such that the camera has to be bang ninety degrees in front of the mammoth mirror. You're in good company though; I didn't know it till I read the explanation in a book. Neither did the Prakash. But like I said, all this almost never happened.

FORUM

Anand Ram of Ahmedabad and Harish Nadkarni of Bombay — both into film-making — maintained that this could easily be done with special effects. One big deal. FX can also commit murders by illusion or blow the death star on Darth Vader's face and a half. Here, on the other hand, are two genuine attempts.

Dear MS,

I am writing to your column for the first time and will therefore avoid half-assed witticisms and stick to plain English (*So may we leave out that first sentence in that case? — MS*). I've thought of a solution to the camera and mirror problem. It's probably wrong but here goes:

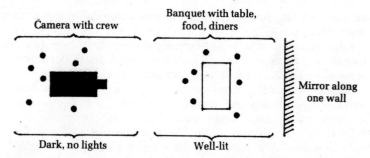

Camera with crew

Banquet with table, food, diners

Mirror along one wall

Dark, no lights

Well-lit

Since the camera and crew are in pitch dark, they will not show up in the mirror. The only images that the camera will record are those of the diners and their reflections. This technique will obviously not work if the camera has to be placed between the diners and the mirror.

Yours,
Argho Sen, New Delhi

Dear MS,

Your problem was quite interesting. If that director had used a mirror in the shot, the solution escapes me. If he used something called 'trick photography', he might have done this.

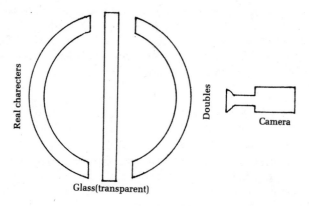

Real charecters

Doubles

Camera

Glass(transparent)

The director may have tried to simulate reflection by placing doubles instead of the real actors (shot from behind in similar garb they would be undetected) while the real actors were on the other side of the glass pane with approximately laterally inverted garb and food. Thus it seemed that there was a mirror in front of the banqueters.

Please let me know if the idea is feasible. I might sell it to G P Sippy for some cash.

Yours sincerely,
Amitabh, SRCC, New Delhi

I don't know if the idea is feasible. Like I mean I guess it could be done but there's this little gotcha about how to laterally invert the faces. I also think you missed the problem somewhat because you don't have to show both sets of diners, just the reflection. But good try, though I don't think we should forward it to the Sippy because then we'll have to see all his characters twice.

The actual solution (at least as reported by Sight & Sound) is that the director took out the mirror from the wall but retained its frame and then shot the sequence through the hole. The "reflection" was the same set of real people seated on the other side. Sexy, no?

(Strikes me now that the problem of lateral inversion of the faces will still be a problem.)

XXXVII

WHOLE IN ONE

People tend to dismiss Calcutta because the streets there have a lot of pot-holes. As if just because of that there's no night life left in the city. This is a very unfair assessment and prejudges the situation without giving the metro a chance to hit back. And hit back it did, fair and squarely, a few years back when a friend of mine called A K Ray was deep in the middle of an extramarital.

Seems like he had — quite reasonably and shrewdly — taken the latest tubelight of his life down one of those deserted by-lanes where the street bulbs are stolen in broad daylight even before they're installed and sold back to the Marxist government in a matter of hours.

And considering Ray and his paramour are not too ... ah ... bright in the skin pigmentation department, they were virtually invisible even unto each other. That's when the city struck.

One moment the comely lass was ensconced with AK — probably making plans for the patter of little feet (incidentally, know what Eskimo couples like to hear? — the chatter of little teeth) — the next he was gone. Just like that. Vanished off the face of the earth. I'm told the maiden was verily distraught and beside herself with consternation and disquiet as she flailed her limbs wildly and vainly in that nightmarish gloom searching and searching for her demon lover. However, no such luck.

It was a few days later when I was visiting AK at a friendly hospital that specializes in repairing detached skeletal elements that the truth came to light. "It was a ghastly experience Mukul," said the broken in-more-senses-than-two man. "There I was putting one foot after the other on solid ground and making a fluid horizontal headway forwards when suddenly the rest of the earth finished. I treaded air for a few seconds before the world swallowed me up."

"Boy you're some asshole AK," I said. "How did you manage to fall into a manhole?"

"Because the stupid manhole cover was not around, that's why."

"Which reminds me," I replied, "do you know why manhole covers are round?"

Of course he threw me out but that was only because he didn't know the answer. The deluded man actually thought they could just as easily be square. The friends I have, I tell you.

FORUM

Dear MS,

As to why manhole covers are round, there are two square reasons. Firstly, a circular cover cannot fall into the hole, like, for instance, a square one can since the diagonal length of the hole is larger than the side's length. Secondly, a round cover can be rolled, and hence, its movement from one place to another is easy.

Yours sincerely,
Shiv Pratap Singh, Jaipur

Dear MS,

It's because there would be some problem of squaring the circle in this problem.

Yours etc,
Ashish Mehta, Ahmedabad

113

Dear MS,

Talking about manholes, can you tell why manholes on industrial boilers are elliptical? (*No, I can't. Besides I didn't even know industrial boilers had manholes. What do they boil in them? Men?* — MS)

Sincerely,
N S Chakravarthy,
IIT-Kanpur

Dear MS,

The boiler is a pressure vessel. For safety the manhole cover is fitted from the inside of the boiler. The manhole is elliptical so that the cover can be inserted or taken out.

Yours sincerely,
Thangavel C, Boiler
Operator, Ahmednagar

Dear MS,

Before the boiler is made into its present shape, its cylindrical surface is a flat, rectangular piece of metal. In this rectangular metal sheet a circular hole is cut to serve as a manhole. When the rectangular sheet is about to form a cylindrical surface, the circular hole becomes distorted into an elliptical hole. This is why industrial boilers have elliptical manholes.

Yours sincerely,
Sanjay Mohan, Aurangabad

XXXVIII

THE HAYSTUCK EFFECT

Ever notice how clever-clever answers have this tendency to blow up in your face? My mug looks like I've just sneezed into an ashtray. And I don't know why I never learn to use an ounce of wisdom instead of a megademic of intelligence. Happened just the other day again. I was going through this book of puzzles to check out on what I could steal when the following intro collided into my gaze.

A phonograph record, I was informed by the printed page, has a total diameter of 12 inches. The recording itself leaves an outer margin of an inch. The diameter of the unused centre of the record is four inches. There are an average of 90 grooves to the inch. And the question was: How far does the needle travel when the record is played?

Hah! I told myself, leaping nimbly into the air like a startled botanist escaping the clutches of a maneating plant in Java, you can't fool me with all this outer margin mumbo-jumbo because the number of grooves per inch spiel has nothing to do with it. The needle doesn't travel around the record; it's the record that turns. The needle is stationary except for its movement towards the centre of the disc. That means, it travels 6 − (2 + 1) = 3 inches.

Howling with glee I turned to the ANS section at the back and swiftly started devouring a can of powdered crow that I keep handy in my hip pocket for occasions just such as these. But I'm not going to tell you why my NEW! IMPROVED! ans was not correct. I want you to suffer too. Want a spoonful?

FORUM

Dear MS,

You're wrong because the needle does not travel in a straight line.

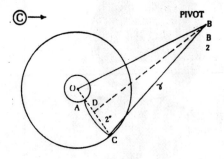

It travels in the arc of a circle, having radius equal to the length of the needle from the pivot and the pivot being the centre.

Thanking you,
Pradeep Raje, New Delhi

116

XXXIX
DEAD ON TIME

I don't know why most people think Canada is just a great big mass of land somewhere to the north of where the US of A finishes and before the polar bears begin their dreary task of trudging about in the snow with only fish on their minds. Ask anyone what a Canadian does and pat comes the answer that he's either a mountie or a maple leaf. Ask them what language they speak and they'll reply in broken French.

Ask them to name any one famous Canadian woman and if they can't answer Mrs Trudeau after a week they'll have a nervous breakdown. This is illiterate gibberish. True, Canada starts where the US of A finishes but then so does Mexico but no one except Mexicans complain about that do they? Far be it my intention to edify people; I'm only thankful they had a poet called Robert Service who, when he wasn't yakking about the great outdoors of his country, was writing things like this:

> Is it not strange that on this common date,
> Two titans of their age, aye of all time
> Together should renounce this mortal state,
> And rise like gods, unsullied and sublime?
> Should mutually render up the ghost,
> And hand in hand join Jove's celestial host?

If you belong to the Lit Major school of thinking and can still sometimes spell Charles Dickens without barging in a j or q somewhere then chances are you've probably guessed which two titans Service is referring to. If you subscribe instead to the radical M.Tech school and you don't know the answer it doesn't matter since you've only got to go through this incarnation peddling n-type transistors and swapping dirty gossip with disk drives about whose motherboard's run away with which ASCII's parity error. Anyway, the guys the guy's yakking about are Shakespeare and Cervantes.

So far so good. Now for the bad news. Both writers died on the same date — 23 April 1616. However, they also died ten days apart. You figure it out; I've got enough problems of my own.

FORUM

53 people got this one right which only proves that there's more gumption out there than inside my skull. But the problem is if I run all of them I'll spill over into "How to Cure Wart Attacks" in Dr Mukesh Batra's homeopathy column on the next page. So the shortest one wins.

Dear MS,

While it is true that Shakespeare and Cervantes died on the same date, the former died in England and the latter in Spain. At that time England was following the Julian calender while Spain had switched to the reformed Gregorian calender. The difference between the two was of ten days.

How about a tougher one next time? I've got enough solutions of my own.

Amol Laha, Calcutta

XXXX

SOME HIKE IT LOT

Using some pretty devious means I have found out that there are only three people in India who subscribe to the *Journal of Recreational Mathematics*. I have also found out their names. And I know for a fact that this journal is not for sale on the stands and is not available at 99 per cent of libraries either. So what does this mean? This means that if those three subscribers whose names I have cold-welded in letters of vanadium to my forehead were to write back answers to the problem I am about to set, then I will torch their missives to soot with oxy-acetylene flames.

Imagine a hiker walking over a horizontal plane, always facing the sun. He walks at constant speed, V, while the sun moves across the sky at a varying speed. The problem is to find the path he traverses if he starts at dawn and stops at dusk. A preliminary survey reveals that his path will be symmetrical about the noon position, where he faces south; at dusk he will be south of his starting point.

FORUM

Dear MS,

The hiker who walks on a horizontal plane with a constant speed, V, facing the sun from dawn to dusk and reaches a point south of his starting point must be a northerner living north of latitude 23½°N. A southerner who lives south of latitude 23½°S will always at dusk reach a point north of his starting point. And the hiker who lives in the tropics which is between latitude 23½°N and latitude 23½°S may reach a point south or north of the point of start depending on the time of the year and, further, on two days in a year, he will reach at dusk the same point from where he started at dawn! I am at Delhi, latitude 28½°N, and hence can never hope to reach at dusk the same point I leave at dawn. But you, Sharma, are at Bombay, (*No way — MS*) latitude 19°N, and are fortunate to reach on two days the same point from where you started at dawn provided you woke up at dawn and walked facing the sun! Now find out for yourself these two days. And if you do not find the correct answer, ask your readers to help you.

Yours sincerely,
Air Vice Marshal (Retd)
S Lakshminarayanan,
New Delhi

Dear MS,

I read the Air Vice Marshal's answer to the hiker's problem. At my age of 60 I cannot agree with it. The hiker who walks on a horizontal plane with a constant speed, V, facing the sun from dawn to dusk and reaches a point south of his starting point must be residing beyond latitude 23½° N. The distance between the two points (starting and ending) is eight times his speed V.

The above proposition can be true between latitude 23½°N and slightly north (i.e., 8V) of the latitude 23½°S while the sun is to the south of the hiker's starting point.

The answer to the question asked by the AVM is that for Bombay (19°N). The above feat cannot be performed from the 4th of June to the 8th of July because on these two days the sun will be over his head, while in between the two dates, the sun will be to the north of him.

Readers may try this themselves.

Yours faithfully,
D R Shirwate, Amravati

Dear MS,

Although Shirwate gives a correct answer to the counter-question I posed, he also gives an incorrect one to the hiker one! Four months are sufficient time to get off the preliminaries and reach the specifics of the solution. Either you publish your final answer or you publish mine. And before that, kindly make a breakfast of eating your words in your statement that you will torch the answers!

If you cannot sing well, so the saying goes, the words in the song are bad. Analogously, if a question is not solvable, there must be something wrong with the question and, most probably with the person who posed the question who in this case is none other than MS of MS. (*Sorry, Mr Air Vice Marshal, like I said and if you had read carefully and understood, you would have known I pinched it from the* Journal of Recreational Mathematics, *but more of this later — MS*) Therefore we question the question and set it in a solvable form. The hiker is required to walk on a horizontal plane with a constant speed V. Now I am a Hiker with a capital H. In July-August 1987 I trekked 300 km to Mount Kailash and lake Manasarovar and back, crossing Lipu Pass (16,000 feet) and Dolma Pass (19,500 feet). I tried to walk on a horizontal plane which, by definition, is a plane tangential to the earth's spherical surface.

P is a point where the horizontal plane touches the earth's surface. A hiker walking on a horizontal plane must have the ability to walk in air! Next, I asked my friend in the air force to fly on a horizontal plane and he said that within a short time the aircraft would reach the outskirts of the atmosphere and, hence, could not be used for movement from dawn to dusk. His advice, instead, was to choose a horizontal surface defined as a spherical surface concentric with the earth's centre. So we modify the question so as not to require the

121

hiker to move on a horizontal plane. Since the earth's surface undulates with hills and dales, rivers and mountains, a walkable horizontal surface is not possible. Instead we can choose a horizontal surface up in the air and fly in it.

As a hiker I note that my speed cannot be a constant when I go on a straight line and return by the same line.

We cannot ask the hiker to go on a path with a 180 degree abrupt change in direction and also keep his speed constant. This is an unreasonable requirement.

If the hiker is at a tropical latitude on a day when the sun is exactly over it, the hiker must move from west to east in the forenoon and from east to west in the afternoon. The apparent speed of the sun on such a latitude is "a cos $\theta 2\pi/24$" where "a" is the earth's radius, "θ" is the latitude and the speed is reckoned in distance per hour. If the afternoon speed is greater than "a cos $\theta 2\pi/24$" he will not be facing the sun but the sun will be on his back after some time. So the speed, V, must be taken smaller than "a cos $\theta 2\pi/24$".

We thus rephrase the hiker question as: "Determine the path of a hiker who moves on a horizontal surface always facing the sun with a constant speed. The exception to constant speed is a tropical latitude where the sun is overhead in which case the hiker's speed at noon is zero and the afternoon speed should be less than "a cos $\theta 2\pi/24$". Here "a" is the earth's radius in km and 'θ' is latitude, and speed is in km per hour.

Yours sincerely,
Air Vice Marshal (Retd)
S Lakshminarayanan AVSM,
New Delhi

Incidentally SL (AVSM), since you were already on this gigantic semantic nitpicking trip, why didn't you take the curvature of spacetime into consideration as well? A bit of quantum tunnelling around never hurt no problem's 'constant speed' or 'horizontal plane'.

Dear MS,

Granting that you are the most intelligent person in the country with the highest IQ, you should still not have commented in a sarcastic manner on SL's letter. You should have respected his age if not anything else. And if you cannot respect your elders while arguing with them, the least that you can do is not to indulge in sarcastic remarks.

In general, your writings are always brash and arrogant. You also write there: "Notwithstanding some stupid detractors..." Now where is the need to call the detractors "stupid"? Agreed that you don't goof off in your column but why show your bad temper? (*Because I'm not paid enough for it — MS*)

Poise, dignity, coolness and humility enhance the personality of man. Brashness and arrogance reduce his stature.

After all, *vidya vinayena shobhate!* (*pata nahin kahan kahan se aa jate hain!* — मु श्र)

Yours truly,
Deepak Deshpande, Nagpur

(*Sounds like my wife. Anyway, let's finish with this damn thing once and for all. Don't know why I started the whole thing.*)

123

ENDGAMES

I

Electricians working with live or potentially live wires generally use the back of their hands (or fingers) to move or check the wires for electricity. Why?

Answer

Since electricity tends to contract your muscles if you touch (the source) with an open palm, the contracting muscles of your palm and fingers make you grip the wire harder and you may not be able to withdraw your hand. On the other hand if you touch it with the back of your fingers, the contracting muscles tend to fold your palm away from the wire.

Hari Shankar, Trivandrum

II

An illiterate man has just died. No question of rigor setting in. His thumb impression is then forced on a faked will. Can the forensic folk find out?

Answer

The answer is no. It is not yet possible to distinguish a post-mortem fingerprint from an ante-mortem fingerprint. I have this from an expert now retired. Salil Kumar Chatterjee, ex-Director, Central Finger Print Bureau of the government. See *Speculation in Fingerprint Identification* by him, privately published in 1981.

Bill Aitken, Mussoorie

III

In the final scene of the film *36 Chowringhee Lane,* Miss Violet Stoneham (MVS) arrives at the house of Samaresh and Nandita (S & N) during a cold Christmas night. Earlier, S&N had hoodwinked MVS into believing that they would not be home. MVS, however, finds party sounds coming from inside.

127

Curious, she wipes condensation off a window pane and peeps in to see a bash in full swing. What's wrong here?

Answer

Because the condensation will be on the other side of the windowpane. So, in reality, Miss Stoneham will not be able to see the inside by wiping the window from the outside.

P K Pal, Surat

IV

What colour does a chameleon turn if you place it on a mirror?

Answer

No idea. But it's a good question though. Thank you.

Ameena S, Madras

V

What is the missing number in the series: 10, 11, 12, 13, 14, 15, 16, 17, 20, 22, 24, 31, 100, ..., 10000, 1111111111111111?

Answer

Here is the complete series: 10, 11, 12, 13, 14, 15, 16, 17, 20, 22, 24, 31, 100, 1000, 10000, 1111111111111111. It is formed by writing 16 in base 16, 15, 14, 13, 12, 11, 10, 9, 8, 7, 6, 5, 4, 3, 2 and 1.

Santha Srinivasan, Bangalore

VI

Why is it that when we measure the speed of a fairly cubical glacier moving down a mountain from the rear with respect to a fixed point of reference, it is always apparently greater than the speed recorded at the front of the glacier?

(*Courtesy: Rajesh Rao, Madras*)

Answer

The higher rate of melting at the front end (because of its lower altitude) makes it appear to be moving at a less faster rate than the rear end (which is at a higher altitude). When the rate of melting at the front end equals the rate of sliding, the glacier appears stationary from the front but moving from the rear.

Shiva Prakash N, Bangalore

VII

What is the quickest way (fewest key depressions) to get an 'E' sign in the display in an ordinary calculator?

(Courtesy: Peter Theobald of no address given.)

Answer

Only two keys need to be pressed. Press the 'division' key followed by the 'equals' key.

Haresh Shenoy, Kanhangad

Just one key is needed. Press the '3' button and hold the calculator upside down!

M A Sreedhar, Mandla

VIII

A box contains two coins that total 55 paise. One of them is not a five paisa coin. What are the coins?

Answer

(A fifty paisa coin and a five paisa coin. Only one of them is not a five paisa coin, remember? — MS)

129

IX

There's this guy driving along San Francisco when he sees a car ahead of him with number plates reading ML-8 ML-8 and starts laughing like crazy because he's reminded of *Alice in Wonderland*. What is the car's colour and make?

Answer

A WHITE VOLKSWAGEN RABBIT! I think the man must have been thinking of the white rabbit in Lewis Carroll's book who kept saying, "I'm late, I'm late."

Debijit Dutta, Kharagpur

X

What will be the date on the first day of the twenty-first century? (Careful here.)

Answer

No, it will not be 1st January, 2000 but 1st January, 2001. That is the reason Arthur C Clarke named his book *2001: A Space Odyssey*.

Anand Bakshi, Kota

XI

A compass rests on a table-top. A magnetized ball rolls around it with the compass's needle pointing to the ball at all times. When the ball has gone completely around the compass, has it gone around the needle?

Answer

I think the magnetic ball has gone around the needle, though it didn't 'see' the other end of it. Suppose a person standing in front of you (who is attracting your attention, of course) makes a complete revolution (or two about-turns), can we take it that you have gone around him?

V Anantharamakrishnan,
Coimbatore

XII

Why does hot water poured from a kettle on to the floor sound different than cold water does?

Answer

Vapour pressure inside hot water is higher than that in cold water which is why there is bubbling when water starts to boil. And that those bubbles comprise steam and not air. So when hot water is poured out, small bubbles are formed which burst, giving rise to a "furrrrrr" sound, whereas cold water, not having any steam bubbles, produces just the sound of water hitting the floor.

Sharad Abhyankar, Wai

XIII

This guy goes to a shop and says, "How much does one cost?" The shopkeeper replies, "Twenty paise." So he asks how much would twelve cost and is told that would be forty paise. "Okay, I'll take eight hundred and thirty one," he says. "That'll be sixty paise," says the shopkeeper. What was the man buying?

Answer

How about wooden or plastic numbers to put on his door to indicate the house number?

Altaf Ahmed, Meerut

XIV

Everyone knows that a compass doesn't point towards the north geographic pole. However, it doesn't point to the north magnetic pole either. So where does it point?

Answer

(*The correct answer is that magnetic compasses don't point to any magnetic pole. What happens is that they align themselves with the*

131

*earth's magnetic field at a given location. Meaning the variation of
the compass may change from year to year. Or to put it another
way, if one were to follow a magnetic compass until she reached the
magnetic pole, her path would not be the most direct one representing
the course a navigator would plot. And in any case, if a compass
needle were free to assume any angle, it would at either of the
magnetic poles, point downward — MS)*

XV

Why does it take longer to raise a flag to half-mast than to
full mast?

Answer

Because to raise it to half-mast it has to be first raised to
full-mast and then lowered to half-mast.

Ashoke Kavi, Bombay

XVI

What happens to the water level in a swimming pool if a
large stone is thrown overboard from a boat which is floating
in the pool? Does the water level rise, fall or remain
unchanged?

Answer

When the stone is in the boat, it manages to displace water
equivalent to its weight (say x units). However, when it is
thrown directly into the water, it manages to displace water
equivalent to its volume (say y units). As the stone will be
(usually) heavier than water, it follows that x is greater than
y. Therefore the water level will go lower. That is, it will fall
when the stone is thrown into the water.

C Rashmikant, Baroda

132

XVII

HEEL is to ACHILLES as BOX is to PANDORA. So,
FOUR-SIDED POLYHEDRON is to TETRAHEDRON as
FOUR-DIMENSIONAL HYPERCUBE is to ... ?

Answer

TESSERACT!

Ravi Chandran, Bombay

XVIII

One can feel the air blow in from every open window of a
moving vehicle. Where does it go out from? You can
demonstrate this to yourself using a strip of paper that a
mass of air does enter the vehicle but no such current of
outgoing air can be felt or discerned.

(*Courtesy: S Keshav, New Delhi*)

Answer

When a car is moving, a column of air enters the car from
the window and, obeying the law of fluid dynamics, forms
big circular eddies in the vicinity and then goes out of the
same window. The person sitting near the open window feels
wind movements of the eddies. The amount of air entering
is exactly the same as that going out.

Ratnesh Mathur,
Ferozpur Cantt

XIX

Given a human being with an inoperable stomach tumour,
and rays which destroy organic tissue at sufficient intensity,
by what procedure can one destroy the tumour using these
rays and at the same time avoid destroying the healthy tissue
which surrounds it?

Answer

Focus the rays on the tumour and then with the tumour as the centre, revolve the machine around the person in a circle. In this way the tumour will constantly get the rays while other tissues only some of the time.

Samuel O'Brien, New Delhi

XX

There exists a perfectly common, valid and grammatically correct sentence in English which, however, can only be spoken and not written, without either changing its meaning, making it ungrammatical or sounding gibberish. Any idea what it is?

Answer

(Consider the words 'to', 'two' and 'too'. You can easily say, "There are three tooz in the English language," by phonetically pronouncing the made up word 'tooz' and convey the information. But what word will you use to write it without giving wrong information? — MS)

XXI

Icicles are usually formed by the snow melting on sloping roofs of cottages. But if it is cold enough for water to freeze (to form icicles) why does the snow melt in the first place?

Answer

Icicles form only on ledges and eaves which do not receive any sunlight. Direct rays of the sun, on the other hand, fall directly on the snow on the roof and melt it even though the temperature is below freezing.

Ambika Nadkarni, Akola

XXII

A hydrogen balloon is rising skywards. Its potential energy is increasing and so is its kinetic energy. Something wrong somewhere?

(Courtesy Pradeep Rage, Amreli)

Answer

The solution lies in the fact that as the balloon rises its potential energy decreases and only the kinetic energy increases. This is so because the balloon's potential energy is not due to the earth's gravitational pull but the buoyant force of the atmosphere on the balloon. Since the weight of the air displaced by it is greater than its own weight the balloon keeps rising and losing its potential energy.

Reetinder, Bombay

The potential energy of an object is minimum in its stable state of equilibrium which, in the case of the balloon, is higher up in the sky where density of the medium is almost equal to the density of the balloon with hydrogen. As such when the balloon is rising, it is going nearer to the equilibrium state and as such its potential energy is decreasing and not increasing.

B B Das, New Delhi

In the two solutions given it is stated that the potential energy (PE) of the balloon is minimum at the top level and maximum at ground level. Actually it is exactly the opposite, being maximum at the top and zero below! With the earth taken as base the PE of a body due to gravitation is due to its position above earth. Its value is equal to m (mass) x g (gravitational force) x h (height above earth). However light a body like rarefied air or hydrogen is, it has PE depending on its height above the ground. At ground level, with zero height, the balloon has no energy at all. What it is subjected to is only a force — the force of buoyancy (Fob) which is equal to the volume of air displaced by the balloon. Force and energy in physics are quite distinct, though in common language this distinction is often confused. Force x distance moved is work or energy (these two are the same in physics, for energy is measured in units of work). Force Fob builds up energy as follows: let Fob overcoming the weight of the balloon (hydrogen + envelope) move through a small height h. Continuing the process, more and more PE is built up with successive increase in height. This goes on till the state

135

is reached where Fob due to the weight of the rarefied displaced air by the balloon diminishes to a value equal to the weight of the balloon so that no further upward movement is possible. Obviously this is the point of maximum PE.

That there is PE at the highest level can also be shown thus: imagine the balloon is made to collapse completely, then the envelope of the balloon would come down; or imagine the surrounding air of the complete balloon is removed, when it will start descending. The movement in both cases shows the presence of kinetic energy. The source of this must be PE.

The mistake of the two solvers lies in their considering buoyancy as energy instead of treating it as a force.

In the above explanation it is assumed that the covering envelope of the balloon is not elastic. What if the material is highly elastic like that of a toy balloon?

K Sukumaran, Kharagpur

XXIII

What would Einstein have been called if he was the 21st child to be born to his parents?

Answer

If Einstein's parents were fecund enough to get into the Guinness by siring 21 siblings — a prodigious feat even by German-Aryan standards — he should have been yclept 'EINUNDZWANZIGSTEIN'.

K Vekatesan, New Delhi

XXIV

Two players agree to empty their wallets on a table. A third party is to count the money in each one. Whoever has the smallest amount of cash will win the contents of the other's wallet. Now each player can say with equal logic, "I stand to lose only what I have, but I can win more than that. The game must be in my favour." Both appear to have the advantage.

But that's paradoxical. How can it be?

Answer

Agreed that you can win more than you can lose, but does that mean that the game is in your favour? After all, if you buy a Maharashtra State lottery ticket, all you can lose is Re 1, whereas you can win Rs 100,000; but does that mean that the lottery is in your favour? Any game is in one's favour if one has a 100 per cent chance of winning, ie one has absolutely nothing to lose. Hence, in this case, the game is strictly in nobody's favour. In fact, if one loses, one has lost whatever one has anyway, which certainly is no favour. Hence there is no paradox.

Mihir Salgarkar, Pilani

XXV

No fun if you take more than two seconds to answer this one. What is the exact opposite of "not in"?

Answer

(No it's not "out" because "out" means "not in". The exact opposite of "not in" is — "in" — MS)

XXVI

To the nearest per cent, the probability that any one person selected at random was born on a Monday is 14. What is the probability, to the nearest per cent, that of any seven persons chosen at random, exactly one was born on Monday?

Answer

0.3965.

Srinath M Sharma, Hyderabad

0.39647.

A Subramaniam, New Delhi

0.3964759.

Vijay Wadhwa, Calcutta

0.39647589043328.

A Subramaniam, New Delhi

XXVII

If you were to inhale helium gas, why would the pitch of
your voice increase?

Answer

Goodbye cruel world, I'm going to sniff helium
So my voice will be shrill when
I scream in delirium.
The question put forth by Mukul Sharma Esquire,
Is, why is that its pitch will be higher?
The required answer — which this mystery unravels—
Is the pitch of sound depends on the speed it travels;
And sound travels faster in Helium than in air
Which is the reason, as far as I am aware.

Rajeshwari Singh, New Delhi

Rajeshwari states, if I correctly read,

That sound travels with greater speed,
In gaseous helium, and therefore
The pitch of her scream will be more!
As a physicist of repute,
It's my duty to dispute
Such a statement's veracity
Since pitch does not change with velocity.
Pitch is a function of frequency;
From any textbook as you can see!

Sridar Ramaswamy,
New Delhi

XXVIII

If H G Wells's invisible man (whose index of refraction
matched the air's index, which is slightly greater than exactly
1, the index for refraction in vacuum) walked into a room,

138

why would you still be able to make out his presence, without him doing anything to make you aware, that is.

Answer

(The correct answer is, the man would be invisible if his index of refraction matched the air's index, which is slightly greater than exactly 1, the index of refraction for vacuum. A greater index would result in some refraction of the rays coming from scenes behind the man, thus making his presence noticeable by the distortion of the images, especially when he walked — MS)

XXIX

Apparently there is only one word in the English language which rhymes with 'orange'. (Hint: it's hyphenated.)

Answer

I think the word you're looking for is "door-hinge".

Gagan Adlakha, New Delhi

XXX

Let an egg float in a glass of water. Turn the tap on over it. For flow rates above some critical value, why will the egg actually rise towards the falling water?

Answer

When the stream from the tap is thin, the surface tension of the sheet of water on the exposed surface of the egg tends to push it down (stretched rubber sheet effect). On the other hand when the tap is opened further, the water falling and the water in the tumbler together form a single column of water. Here the law of buoyancy predominates and the egg tends to rise. Correct?

L A Ramanathan, Mysore

(Actually, according to the great American science communicator and puzzle fiend, Jearl Walker: "Apparently nothing more than a description

139

has been published on this demonstration. Why not try experimenting with it? What is the pressure just above and just below the egg? Does turbulence matter? Suppose an egg that would float in static water were in a narrow, horizontal water jet. Would the egg move upstream in the jet?" — MS)

XXXI

How can two girls who were born at the same time, on the same day of the same month, in the same year and of the same parents, not be twins?

Answer

They are two of a set of triplets. Or quadruplets. Or Quintuplets. Etc.

Sanjay N Kulkarni, Baroda

XXXII

A certain person lived for many years to a ripe old age. But he celebrated his birthday only a few times since his birthdays "stopped coming" (as he put it). He was right. What is the explanation?

(*Courtesy: V Chandran, Bombay*)

Answer

He was born on February 30, 46 BC (at that time there was a February 30). In 45 BC, Julius Caesar started the year from January instead of from March. He also named the seventh month 'July' in his own honour. Since July was named after Caesar, it could not possibly have less days than other months, so he subtracted one day from February and added one day to July to bring it to 31 says. Julius Caesar also introduced the concept of the "leap year". Hence in the "Julian Calendar" (named after him, of course) every year divisible by four had an extra day added in February. Hence 44 BC being a leap year, had a February 30 and so our hero could celebrate his birthday. On March 15, 44 BC Julius

140

Caesar was assassinated and soon thereafter Octavian became Caesar and assumed the title 'Augustus Caesar'. Shortly afterwards he emulated his predecessor by naming the eighth month 'August' in honour of himself. He also upgraded August by adding one day to it so that it had 31 days. Naturally he had to subtract one day from February to compensate for this. Incidentally, the Romans considered February to be an unlucky month and were quite pleased when it was made shorter and shorter. So now February had 28 days, and 29 days in leap year. So our hero could never ever celebrate any more birthdays on February 30 since they simply "stopped coming"!

V Chandran, Bombay

XXXIII

Can one make a hole in the middle of an ice cube by focussing the rays of the sun with a magnifying lens into its centre?

Answer

(I had received a neat little answer to this one but I can't find it. Will the person who sent it in please ditto a repeat? — MS)

XXXIV

Suppose all organisms and animals inhabiting earth instead occupied a planet with one tenth the atmospheric pressure as earth. Then a horse-drawn carriage driver wouldn't wield the same power of authority with his whip. Why?

(Courtesy: Deepak Somaya, Bombay)

Answer

If we assume that it is the crack of the whip which frightens or goads the horses and not the physical pain of the lash itself then indeed our authority over horses would be diminished. The reason is because the crack of a whip is actually a mini sonic boom produced when the tip exceeds

141

the speed of sound. On a planet as described, the speed of sound would be far greater.

Vivian Lobo, Pune

XXXV

When Mike was twice as old as Judy was when Mike was three times as old as Judy was when Mike was as old as Judy is now, Judy was half as old as Mike was when Judy was half as old as Mike is now.

The ages are in whole numbers. How old are these two?

Answer

Mike and Judy are respectively 62 and 39 years of age. The problem posed is algebraically expressed as

$$M - J = \{14J - 8M\} - \{M - (J - M/2)\}$$

taking into account that the difference in their ages should be the same at any point of their lives. The expression reduces to

$$62J = 39M$$

(J and M being their present ages) which is an indeterminate equation capable of many solutions, the smallest integral values being $M = 62$ and $J = 39$.

D K Mishra, Ranchi

XXXVI

There's Anu, Bini and Rita. Each belongs either to the Tee family whose members always tell the truth or the El family whose members always lie. Anu says, "Either I belong or Bini belongs to a different family from the other two." Whose family do you know the name of?

142

Answer

Suppose Anu belongs to the Tee family. Now if Bini belongs to the Tee family, Anu's statement is false. So Bini belongs to the El family. Rita may belong to either of the families.

Suppose next that Anu is a member of the El family. Then Anu's statement is false only if Bini belongs to the El family and Rita belongs to the Tee family.

Hence, whichever be Anu's family, Bini belongs to the El family.

Shiv Pratap Singh,
Thakarda, Rajasthan

XXXVII

Where will you reach if you if you keep going north-west as far as you can?

Answer

I think what will happen is that one will slowly and concentrically spiral towards, and into, the North Pole.

Navin Kishore Singh,
Chandigarh

XXXVIII

If 1904 was a leap year and if leap years recur every four years then why wasn't 1900 a leap year?

Answer

For a year ending with two zeros it should be divisible by four hundred to be a leap year. Thus 1900 was not a leap year.

Mahesh Bhatt, Mangalore

The solar year consists of 365 days, 5 hours, 48 minutes, 48 seconds. But for the sake of convenience it is taken as 365 days. But this is 11 minutes, 12 seconds more than the actual.

To rectify this Pope Gregory **XII** made century years leap years only once in four centuries; so that whilst 1700, 1800 and 1900 were to be ordinary years, 2000 would be a leap year. This modification brought the Gregorian system into such close exactitude with the solar year that there is only a difference of 26 seconds, which amounts to a day in 3323 years!

Atul Samalir, New Delhi

XXXIX

Which is the only bone in the human body which does not articulate with any other bone? (Try this one on a doctor sometime; they look hilarious when they don't know the answer.)

Answer

(It's the u-shaped hyoid bone in the neck which supports the tongue — MS)

XL

Two trains A and B start simultaneously from Bombay and Calcutta bound for the other city with no stops in between. A travels at 100 kmph while B travels at 75 kmph. If the distance between the two cities is 2000 km, which train will be further from Bombay when they meet?

Answer

Obviously, wherever they meet they will be at the same place together, so that they will be equally far away from Bombay or Calcutta.

Hutokshi Contracter, Girgaun

XLI

Which of these go clockwise and which anti?

1. *Skaters in a rink*

144

2. *Monopoly pieces*
3. *The chariot race in* Ben Hur
4. Hula Hoops
5. The Nazi swastika
6. Merry-go-rounds
7. Bidding in bridge
8. Water draining from a sink
9. Tornadoes
10. Revolving doors

Five out of ten correct is good.

Answer

(All of them generally go anticlockwise, with the exception of bridge and Monopoly — both table games. The reasons are obscure and no two anthropologists agree on why humans, whenever setting themselves in rotational motion, prefer the anti-direction. On the other hand, it is interesting to note that when humans provide impetus to objects the direction is normally clockwise — MS)

XLII

It's easy to get a hardboiled egg inside a bottle. All you do is drop a burning taper inside the bottle and place the egg on the mouth and wait. But how do you get a hardboiled egg inside a bottle *with* its shell? Or for that matter, how can you get the insides of an egg out without touching its shell?

Answer

Immerse the egg — shell and all — in vinegar for a couple of days till it becomes soft. Then use the same method as for a hardboiled egg without its shell.

O K Shaj, Madras

To get the insides of an egg out without touching the shell, you have to get mother hen to do the job. Let her sit on it, and when it's time enough the inside will come out on its own, outside.

G M Srinivasa Bhatt, Madras

145

XLIII

Why does a bruise appear bluish-purple when the haemor-
rhaging blood beneath the hurt surface is red?

Answer

God knows.

XLIV

If you drew the cardinal points of the compass at the ends
of two intersecting arrows but substituted east for west and
vice versa, where on earth would that drawing be correct?

(*Courtesy: Ponnappa, Bangalore*)

Answer

In a mirror!

Reshmi Anand, Hissar

On the ceiling!

Thomas ("The Boy")
George, Dhanbad

XLV

Only one five letter word is found in verse - - - - - - -,
chapter - - - - - -, Book of - - - - - - - - - - in the Bible.

What is it?

(*Note: the number of dashes equals the number of letters in the words
concerned.*)

Answer

The only five-letter word was "found" in the Book of
Revelation, chapter twenty, and verse fifteen.
    To find it you made me read from Genesis to Revelation.

Pradip Mahanty, Cuttack

146

There are only three books in the Bible with a ten-letter name: *Chronicles, Colossians* and *Revelation.*

Chronicles are in two parts, so put it away.

Colossians contains only four chapters: one, two, three and four, none of which are six-lettered numbers.

So it is outnumbered.

Revelation has twenty-two chapters, of which eleven, twelve and twenty are six-lettered.

In chapter eleven there are 19 verses, in chapter twelve, 17 and in chapter twenty there are 15 verses.

Of these verses only 15 and 16 are seven-lettered numbers.

Verses 15 and 16 of chapters eleven and twelve have more than one five-lettered word.

But in verse 15, chapter twenty there is only one five-lettered word.

The word is "found".

AKP, no address given

XLVI

Why do photographs of watches and clocks in advertisements almost always show the time as ten minutes past ten?

Answer

(No, it's not because that is when Abraham Lincoln died.

Let me quote the Dictionary of Misinformation: "A persistent myth has it that display clocks are set (so) because that is the hour Abraham Lincoln died or, sometimes, the hour at which he was shot.

Actually Lincoln was shot shortly after 10.00 p.m. and died at 7.30 the next morning."

The obvious reason is that 10.10 is symmetrical and leaves space at the top and bottom for the lettering to be read — MS)

XLVII

Humayun was Akbar's father's what?

Answer

Humayun was Akbar's father's name!

Yusuf Noorani, Bombay

XLVIII

Observed the wheels of a train?

Two wheels, one on either side, are mounted on the same axle. Logically, therefore, as the train travels along a curved track, there should be some slip between the inner wheel and the railway line. But this does not happen. Why?

Answer

The wheels are coned (1 in 20 to be precise.) While negotiating a curve, the outer wheel rolls more on the axle end of the wheel than the inner wheel. As a result, the portion of the outer wheel in contact with the rails is of a larger dia than the portion of the inner wheel riding on the rail. Thus while negotiating a curve, the outer wheel rolls and covers a larger distance than the inner wheel for the same rpm. Hence there is no slip. You can observe the same effect by taking a tumbler and rolling it on a flat surface. You will find that the tumbler does not roll straight but rolls in a curve.

N Bhattacharyya, Hyderabad

XLIX

Two men have to race their horses from A to B. The winner is the man whose horse comes in last. Whoever tries to deliberately ride slow automatically loses. How can we have a winner?

Answer

The answer is that the two men should exchange horses. Each riding the other's horse, that is. This way, each will try to be the first so that the other (and, therefore, his horse) comes in last.

Preeti Kashyap, Anywhere

L

When you dip your fingers inside a tin of biscuits why does the air feel cooler?

Answer

(A) I bought a tin of biscuits and opened it. It was full. There was no room to dip my fingers in.

(B) I took out a tin of biscuits from the fridge (partly used). The air inside was certainly cooler than the outside room temperature.

(C) I kept that second tin closed on the table for four hours and then opened it again. Yes the air in the tin was still cooler than the outside air because the tin and biscuits warmed up better than the inside air (due to poorer conduction).

George B Pradhan,
Vishakhapatnam

LI

A person has only a visiting card to use for writing a full letter in normal sized handwriting. How does (s)he do it?

(Courtesy: Bill Aitken, Mussoorie)

Answer

I am writing a full sized letter in normal handwriting to you on a visiting card. Only, it has been split into five sheets each like this one. All you have to do is make the card damp and then use a penknife to split the card into its constituent paper sheets.

P S Ravikanth, Hyderabad

LII

The sound of cracking knuckles has nothing to do with the bones of the fingers. What does it have to do with?

Answer

Pulling the fingers causes a sudden release of tiny gas bubbles in the fluid between the bones which accounts for the noise.

It takes a while before the pressure can be built up again for recracking the knuckles.

Ranbir Singh, Okhla

LIII

If I say that I know a man who once married his widow's sister, then am I wrong? Actually I'm not. How?

Answer

(Simple. Say you married A, who subsequently died. Then say you married A's sister B and after a while you yourself died. This makes B your widow. So, it would be quite correct to say that you had once married your widow's sister — MS)

LIV

Can a ball (sphere) roll on ice (zero friction)?

(Courtesy: Vivek Ranjan, Kanpur)

Answer

A ball can certainly roll on ice provided you spin it beforehand. Since there is no external torque acting on it (since no friction), the angular momentum of the ball is conserved. Therefore the sphere should, theoretically, continue to roll on forever.

U Raghavendra, Kurnool

LV

Why, if you were to rip out this page and crumple it and then lay the crumpled wad back in the book, would at least one point on the page be directly over its original position?

Answer

The wad covers a smaller portion of the original area and the remaining part is irrelevant. Let us now remove from the wad the paper corresponding to this irrelevant part. Now the area covered by the wad becomes smaller, giving rise to a fresh irrelevant portion. If we go on repeating these removals, one possibility is that the wad will be reduced to a point above its corresponding point.

S L Pathi, Rajahmundry

LVI

If our knees bent the other way what would be the shape of chairs?

Answer

Another good question. Thank you again.

Ameena S, Madras

LVII

There's a six letter word in English which has three 'Y's and no other vowel; including semis like H or W or even J. Only pure and simple consonants.

Good luck.

Answer

Syzygy *n.* **1.** (Astron.) conjunction or opposition, esp. of moon with sun. **2.** pair of connected or correlated things. [f. LLf.Gk *suzugia* (*suzugos* yoked, paired, f. as SY- + *zugon* yoke; see -Y)]

Yours etc,
Nalini Parekh, Bombay

LVIII

Even though everyone knows −40° Fahrenheit is the same as −40° Centigrade why is it that you can never prove it with an ordinary thermometer?

151

Answer

You gave it away by saying "ordinary" because we all know ordinary thermometers have mercury in them and mercury freezes at –39 Centigrade.

Raghu Raman, Tirupur

LIX

Why is blood pressure measured on the arms and not on the leg?

Answer

The problem of tying the cuff on the thigh is fraught with mechanical problems, and in females there may be modesty problems.

Dr Pradip Cherian, Ludhiana

The arteries involved in the arm are more superficial than those in the thigh or calf and, hence, are easily palpitated.

Dr Ajit M Patil, Solapur

When we measure the blood pressure (bp) on the arm, our aim is to measure the bp at the level of the heart. In fact, the bp at the brachial artery gives us a near enough value of the bp at the site of the outlet of the left ventricle; ie at the aortic valve. Incidentally, bp can also be measured on the legs, for instance in people with no hands, or, in very small children if the cuff size is too large for their hands.

Dr Jagjit Singh Batra,
New Delhi

LX

How can one make out from a photograph whether it's a full moon partially eclipsed or a normal moon which is not full?

152

Answer

In a normal moon which is not full there will be a faint, fine outer line completing the circle. This will not be there in an eclipsed moon.

Ragini and Padmini Katiyar,
Jullundur